NEWER ANGLES ON SQUASH

Newer Angles on Squash

R. B. HAWKEY

FABER & FABER
3 Queen Square, London

First published in 1973
by Faber and Faber Limited
3 Queen Square London WC1
Printed in Great Britain by
The Bowering Press Plymouth
All rights reserved

ISBN 0 571 10259 x

Contents

List of Illustrations

Introduction

A little over ten years ago, I was asked whether I would care to write a book on Squash. It happened to be rather a busy time for me, but I had felt for a long while that something more was needed on a Squash player's bookshelves beyond the purely technical instruction manuals, containing elaborate pictures of how someone in the 1920s gripped his racket, and masses of diagrams of foot positions for all the various strokes, like a *Radio Times* hand-out for the 'Come Dancing' series. I had always felt that the speed of the game, and the lightness of the racket and ball, made improvisation more necessary and easier to achieve than in most sports, and that it would be a good idea to aim at making people think more about tactics and the mental approach to the game rather than merely the technical details of stroke production. At the same time, I hoped that a little informality and personal reminiscence would add interest and prevent the book becoming too much of a textbook. And so *New Angles on Squash* was duly published.

My publishers, being gluttons for punishment, encouraged me to write two further books covering coaching in depth. One, aimed at the teenage beginner, was called *Your Book of Squash* in the well-known *Your Book of . . .* series, and the other, directed at the average player, was *Improving your Squash*. *New Angles on Squash* sold out and is now replaced by its successor *Newer Angles on Squash*.

One might think at first that an author, when producing a revised version of a book, would repeat much of what he wrote the first time, and indeed in some places it is very difficult not to do this. For example, the rules and the methods of Marking and Refereeing have not altered a great deal, and one cannot very profoundly vary the hints on how to call the score! However, I think I can dispel fears that this book is merely vain repetition by explaining what I have been doing in the Squash world in the decade since *New Angles on Squash* appeared.

In 1962 I was master in charge of Squash and Cricket at Merchant Taylors' School, which up to then was my only experience of coaching. I had been Technical Adviser of the S.R.A. for a few years, but the boom in building courts had not fully got under way, and the Australian ball was still many years ahead. My international playing career had ended in 1960 (about time too, as I was thirty-seven then!), but I was still playing in the Bath Cup 1st Division and in county matches. And of course, *New Angles* was my first venture into writing.

In 1972 I am still master in charge of Squash and Cricket at Merchant Taylors', but a few years after *New Angles* was finished, the S.R.A. decided to appoint a Director of Coaching, and I was fortunate enough to land the job. This caused me to give a great deal more thought to the whole business of coaching, and, I am glad to say, brought me into close contact with that great gentleman of Squash, Jack Giles, from whom I have learned a vast amount. As a result of my duties in this role, I have lectured and taught at many classes, courses, centres and clubs over the years, and feel I know a great deal more about coaching now than I did ten years ago.

Similarly with Refereeing and Marking; this is now one of the subjects for which the Director of Coaching is responsible, and again entails lecturing and examining would-be officials for the appropriate certificate. I have also been fortunate enough to referee many top matches, including the Britain *v*. Australia match at Edgbaston Priory, and the final of the world singles championship at the Lansdowne, when the international team and individual events were held in this country in 1969. I am still in charge of the technical advice branch of the S.R.A. It has proved a very interesting and rewarding (if at times exacting and worrying) ten years, as the courts have gone up, new materials and equipment have been introduced and the ball has been changed. I am still playing Bath Cup 1st Division Squash, being wheeled in my bath chair to matches by my faithful henchmen, and it was only a year or two ago that I last appeared for Middlesex in the inter-county championship; so I feel I have kept in touch with current players and their views as far as I can. Finally, this is now my fourth book, and I have written articles regularly in the various Squash magazines. Consequently, I think the years since my first very nervous attempt at writing a book on the game have given me the opportunity and material for writing a further book completely different from its predecessors, and one which I hope is interesting and stimulating.

Certainly, as the game has boomed, the interest in all branches of it has also developed. There are many more beginners around nowadays requiring basic instruction; there are more would-be coaches and more would-be referees and markers, and there is a tremendous need for both coaches and officials; and, of course, there are more players interested in improving their game and learning something about its history and how it is organized.

If this book reflects the pleasure I have had from Squash, and helps other enthusiasts to increase their own enjoyment of the game, I shall be very well satisfied.

1: Squash and You

I get more than a little tired of people commenting on how incredible the boom in Squash is. Certainly the statistics of court building, sale of equipment, demand for courts and number of players are quite staggering. But what always seems more incredible to me is that it did not happen years ago. Squash has so much in its favour, especially in countries like Great Britain, Sweden and Northern European countries in general, that it really amazes me that it has only recently become 'big business'. After all, if the game flourishes in countries like Australia, South Africa, Egypt and other hot areas, where the climate must tend to push people towards the beaches and not into little four-walled ovens, how much more should it flourish in countries where it is often too wet for Cricket and Tennis, too foggy or frosty for the outdoor winter games, and where the winter evenings seem to start about an hour after lunch?

Of course its development was held back by lack of courts and the expense of building new ones, but it seems that once the really urgent demand was there, the courts were built, and have gone on being built. The 'snowball' began ten or fifteen years ago and gradually developed into the avalanche of today. Unlike some transient crazes, it seems certain that Squash is here to stay, and indeed to increase, as there is absolutely no sign of the avalanche slowing up yet.

Basically, Squash has the advantage over the outdoor games of being playable in all weathers throughout the year, at any time of the day or night. It is relatively cheap to play,

14

as the racket costs less than a Tennis racket, and only one ball is necessary. This, compared to the outlay necessary for a golfer or cricketer, is very reasonable. It has an advantage over games like Rackets, Real Tennis and various forms of Fives in that it has a great many competitions at all levels, leading to county and international representation, overseas tours and even 'world' events. Clearly it cannot be long before Squash becomes an Olympic event, which is more than one can hope for these other games, enjoyable as they are. As a result, the young, ambitious player tends to opt for Squash rather than other forms of sport. Also, it has the advantage of offering a chance of getting a great deal of exercise in the minimum of time; half an hour at lunchtime or on the way home, once or twice a week, will reduce considerably the strain on a businessman's waistcoat buttons, and because it is possible to play at any time, people with jobs that call for unusual hours of work can fit in a game whenever their particular free time happens to be.

It is also a pleasanter way of training for other games than running round the block; many Rugger and Soccer clubs encourage their members to play Squash, and indeed it not only improves their fitness and wind, but makes them think quickly and develop agility as well as stamina.

I suppose, however, that the answer to my own bewilderment about why the boom has happened now and not before lies largely in the way modern life has developed. People lead more hectic lives, and need to cram their exercises into shorter periods, whenever a spare half-hour presents itself. Perhaps modern life makes people aggressive and this can be (more or less!) satisfactorily catered for by letting them knock hell out of a little black ball, in a desperate and determined attempt to beat an opponent. Perhaps, also, Women's Lib has had an effect; no longer is the wife or girl friend of a games player quite so content to trail round a golf course, prepare interminable teas or freeze on a touch line. She is, however, prepared to sip gin in a comfortable Squash club lounge, and even learn to play herself, and she certainly

15

approves of being separated from the current object of her affections for a shorter period than most games demand.

So much for the various reasons why people decide to take up the game in the first place. Having done so, two other relevant and encouraging factors emerge; the first is that it is a much easier game for a beginner to pick up, and in no time at all he or she can be having quite long and enjoyable rallies and feeling that this is a very rewarding game to play. Secondly, wherever one removes to in the U.K., and in an ever-increasing number of countries abroad, one can find facilities not too far away for continuing to play Squash.

For those interested in how it all began, I will try to trace its development from the unofficial knock-about in an open-air yard to the sophistication of a major tournament sport played all over the world. Presumably the embryo was formed about 1850; rumour has it that it began at Harrow School, and it is clear that it was a direct offshoot from the game of Rackets, because the markings of the court, the phraseology and many of the rules are similar. It seems likely that it was begun by boys, waiting for their turn to get on the Rackets court, knocking up in the area outside it, where the noise of the hard ball against the walls and the risk of broken windows persuaded authority to decree that if this practice were to continue, a soft ball must be substituted. Thus it became a 'squashy' type of Rackets. Obviously, at this stage, there were no regulations about just how 'squashy' the ball should be, and presumably any old soft ball would do, but clearly the lads playing this new game discovered that they could now produce shots which were not possible with the genuine hard Rackets ball. This must have intrigued them to such an extent that they followed it up at home in the holidays, and played in any suitable form of outbuilding. Maybe, too, the genuine Rackets enthusiasts welcomed the chance of keeping their eyes in with this new game while away from school and with no Rackets court available. Certainly, towards the end of the century, the first genuine Squash courts, designed especially for the game, began to be built at some country houses. There were no official dimensions or markings, but the various courts do not seem to have differed too widely, and at the turn of the century a London West End club, the Bath Club, actually built a Squash court for its members. The men who designed and built this court must have indeed been far-sighted, for when the authorities finally laid down the exact measurements and dimensions, they took as their model this original court at the Bath Club, and it has proved over the years to be a very good decision.

The first official mention in print that the game seems to have received was in a coaching manual of court games published in 1874, in which there is a passing reference in the chapter on Rackets to 'squash' rackets—the inverted commas and small letters are from the original, and not mine. By 1890, to judge from another publication of that date, the game had begun to be established, and the private courts built. It was still very much a Public School, University and West End club game, and indeed remained so to far too great an extent until very recently.

The sad thing about these early days was that decisions about what final size the court should be, and what type of ball would eventually prove most acceptable were not taken before the game was exported to America. In this country, the game was governed by a sub-committee of the Tennis and Rackets Association, and remained so right up to 1929, but in the United States, a Squash Rackets Association was formed in 1907, presumably because there was no T. and R.A. to act as a parent body. They, most unfortunately, settled for a court which is $2\frac{1}{2}$ feet narrower and 1 foot longer than our own, and with different heights for the out-of-court lines on all walls. They also adopted a solid rubber type of ball, and the resulting game, while an excellent one, is very different from our own. Those who have seen or played both will understand the famous way of describing the difference between the two codes; the British game is the one in which two gentlemen chase a small black ball around a court, and the American game is the one where the small black ball chases the two gentlemen!

In any case, the game got away to a fast start in the States, and indeed their first championship was held in 1906, even before the formation of their S.R.A.; and Canada was not far behind, forming their Association in 1911. Of the countries who decided to play the English type of Squash, the South Africans were the first by a very long way to form an official association; they did so in 1910.

In England, things did not move further than friendly games and club championships until after the 1914–18 war. Then in 1920 the first Professional championship was held, and was won by Charles Read. This did not become an annual event until the 1930s, but was on a challenge basis, and Read was not in fact challenged again until 1928, when he again won. On both occasions he beat Johnson, the Pro at the Royal Automobile Club, and the scores were interesting. At that time, two matches were played, one on the home court of each player, and on both occasions Read won with the greatest of ease on his own Queen's Club court and lost narrowly at the R.A.C. It appears that even in those days there was considerable difference between hot and cold courts!

The following year, 1921, the ladies held their first Amateur championship, and the men's Amateur began a year later, in 1922. Both continued as annual events from then on, and, apart from the war, have been held regularly since their inception. It is interesting to note that up to and including 1925 the scoring was as in Rackets, and games were up to 15, whereas from 1926 onwards, the scoring was as it is today, with games up to 9 points. I wonder why, three years before the T. and R.A. ceased to be the governing body of the game, the change was made, and whether it had any effect on the play; certainly the year before the change came, in the final of the amateur, Cazalet beat Palmer-Tomkinson 15–8, 12–15, 18–17, and the following season Palmer-Tomkinson beat Cazalet 9–5, 9–7, 7–9, 9–6. Obviously there was little to choose between the two, and any slight difference that the change made could well have swung the balance.

In 1929 the Squash Rackets Association was formed, and the game became 'independent' in this country for the first time. The following year, the S.R.A. began the Open Championship, which was virtually the world singles championship right up until the International Federation had been formed and the team and individual events organized every few years by the Federation included a genuine world singles event.

Because Charles Read had retained his Professional championship in 1928, he was designated as the 1930 Open Champion, and was challenged by Donald Butcher, then the Pro at the Conservative Club. Butcher won both matches by 3 games to 0, the championship being played, like the Professional, on a home and away basis until 1947. Butcher won it once more, but from then on the roll of honour in the Open became the preserve of Egyptians and Pakistanis. From Don Butcher's win in 1931 right through to Barrington's victory in 1966 only one British player won the Open, Jim Dear in 1938. The man who monopolized the 1930s was Amr Bey, the famous Egyptian amateur, who was clearly the greatest player before 1939. He won the Open five consecutive years, and the Amateur six times altogether. Meanwhile the Professional champion was Jim Dear, who won the title from Don Butcher in 1935 and held it until the war, and in fact even won it again in 1949, a last British fling before the Pakistani domination.

As far as team events were concerned, there were international matches between the wars, but nowhere near the innumerable series that are held today. The first Great Britain side went over to Philadelphia and took part in the matches for the Lapham Trophy. This was a trophy to be played for annually between the U.S.A. and Canada, and in the 1923 and 1926 seasons the British tourists took part, coming second in 1923 and winning in 1926. Perhaps a little surprisingly, Canada has won this trophy some seventeen times, over a third of the occasions on which it has been played. Apart from these two occasions, Great Britain entertained the U.S.A. in England three times, in 1924, 1928 and 1935, winning 5–0 in all three matches. It had now become clear that genuine international competition between the two codes of Squash was not possible. The Ladies continue to compete with the U.S.A. for the Wolfe-Noel Cup, which began in 1933 and has continued every few years since then. The point about the futility of competition at this level is best brought out by an analysis of the results in the first sixteen Wolfe-Noel Cup matches played between 1933 and 1968. In the eight matches played in England, the British team won 5–0 on every occasion, a total of 40 matches to 0. Of the eight played in the U.S.A., Britain actually won three matches, and the individual results showed, surprisingly, a 21–19 advantage to the visitors.

The reason for this is that the U.S.A. game, an excellent one, deservedly popular in North America, has not the range of shots of the English game, and when one of our players goes to America, he has the comparatively easy task of polishing up some of the shots which are in his normal English repertoire, and forgetting others, whereas his American counterpart has not only got to adapt his normal game, but also to learn completely new shots. Also, of course, the English ball (on our larger court) demands that players move much further into the corners of the court in order to retrieve it, and because of its comparative slowness, the English rallies are much longer. For both of these reasons, a perfectly fit American player might easily become exhausted in England, whilst the more staccato American rallies would be no strain on a normal English player's strength or wind.

Obviously much has been lost by this difficulty of getting worthwhile international matches against the Americans, and one hopes that, under the International Federation's guidance and encouragement, the future may see the resumption of matches which provide keen and meaningful competition.

At home, the only international series to be begun before

the war were England *v.* Scotland and Scotland *v.* Ireland, both in 1937, but Europe just managed to get in on the act in 1939, when Sweden dealt somewhat faithfully with Denmark by 9 ties to 3 in Stockholm!

The inter-county championship began in 1929, the Oxford *v.* Cambridge match in 1925, and the annual Amateurs *v.* Professionals affair in 1931. The Services began their individual titles in the mid-twenties, and it is always amusing to see names recurring every few years with an upward movement in rank. At least one can follow their progress, unlike some of the ladies, who cloak their activities by changing their names—in some cases more than once! I am always intrigued by the list of winners of the Civil Service championship. For all the early years the branch of the service is put in brackets after the winner's name, and the Foreign Office, the Ministries of Agriculture and Works, the Treasury, Post Office, etc., all get honourable mention. A sinister note has now crept in—the branch is omitted. Is this because the gentlemen concerned are on tremendously secret work of national importance, or because they are so busy concentrating on their Squash that they do no work at all! What a pity they, unlike the Services, miss out on having their seniority and advancement recorded for posterity. Surely a simple figure giving the length, thickness or quality of their office carpets would suffice!

In 1950 the game received a very rude shock indeed—Hashim Khan arrived in England and Squash has never been the same! I recall Donald Butcher going along to see Hashim's first practice session at the Junior Carlton against the Pro there, a cousin of his I believe, the very popular Abdul Bari. When he came back to Hampstead there was a glazed look in Don's eyes, and when asked what he thought of Hashim, he remarked, 'Well, I've seen him do everything today except run round the out-of-court line, and he'll probably do that tomorrow.' This gives some idea of the fantastic agility and speed of Hashim, and, to almost the same degree, of his brother Azam and cousin Roshan. There was great

21

excitement to see whether the graceful stroke-playing champion, Karim, could withstand the bustling, bashing challenge of Khan. The final lasted only thirty-three minutes, and although Karim was not fully fit, according to reports, there could be no doubt that the whirlwind from Pakistan could sweep all before him. It is worth quoting from the account of this final in the S.R.A. handbook of the following year, in which it says: 'Khan's speed of stroke and retrieving were such as to justify the remark of one spectator after a particularly wonderful "get", "But that's not possible." The score was 9–5, 9–0, 9–0. The king was dead, long live the king.

From then on a Khan held the Open Championship until Taleb of Egypt won in 1962. Hashim won the title a total of seven times, Azam four times and Roshan and Mohibullah, a nephew, and not really in the same class, once each. Roshan's win in 1956 was a wonderful feat; he had fought against injury most of his career, but on this occasion he was fully fit, and added to the normal Khan speed a fine range of shots. Hashim and Azam could no doubt play any shot they wished, but too often their games were tremendously hard hitting affairs played at a fantastic speed, with only nick winners being attempted. Roshan had a fine touch and used his range of shots to a far greater extent, and I personally enjoyed watching him play more than the other two. At least there was some uncertainty about the result when Roshan played, whereas it soon became apparent that Hashim and Azam were virtually playing exhibition matches, even in major tournament finals, and Hashim would inevitably win in the fifth game. One felt that Hashim could have won very easily had he pulled out all the stops, but decided that the spectators wanted to see a long match. Maybe at first this was true, but after a while spectators became a little bored with these games and would, I think, have liked to have seen Hashim win as convincingly as he could. After about an hour and a half of the speed and noise of a Khan battle, one left the court feeling a little like a drum that has been through an Aldershot tattoo! Nevertheless, the game had been changed, and the way paved for the Barringtons and Hunts to come. Fitness, speed and stamina had taken over from the gentler skills, and only the full-time player, whether he calls himself an Amateur or a Professional, can now cope with the demands of the game. No genuine Amateur doing a normal job can train sufficiently or practise long enough to acquire the physical condition and the consistency of stroke play to compete at the top level.

After the Khans, there was bound to be an anti-climax. Mahibullah was never in the class of the three elder Khans, although too fast for the rest of the field in 1962. Thereafter Taleb won the Open title three times before Barrington's win in 1966, but both were pedestrian compared with the Khans. The only player who might have won points on merit off Hashim at his best, in my opinion, is Geoff Hunt from Australia. He moves extremely easily around the court, albeit without the explosive spurts and the squeal of brakes I always associate with Hashim, and has fine shots. However, I have seen him tired after a mere two hours with Barrington, and I doubt if Hashim would have removed his sweater by then!

To revert to the administrative side, the S.R.A. remained the governing body of the English type of game until the International Squash Rackets Federation was formed in January 1967, after over a year of discussion and debate among the leading Squash playing countries. Initially there were seven founder members, Great Britain, South Africa, Egypt, Australia, India, Pakistan and New Zealand, but since then the U.S.A. and Canada have been elected 'back dated' founder members, and other countries are joining almost yearly as full or associate members. The I.S.R.F. is now the governing body and is responsible for any changes in the rules and for organizing the world team and individual championships as regular events.

The S.R.A., however, is still the governing body for Great Britain and is responsible for running the game in this country. With the game booming as it is, the administration is hard put to it to try and meet the many calls on its time and finances. The days when Squash was a minor sport, which could be run by a Secretary who could type, are long since gone. Squash is now a 'major' sport with all the advantages and problems, rewards and headaches that that entails. The Association needs support and finance, and, to keep the game flourishing, it is hoped that a sufficient number of the new players will be prepared to do some work for the game and join the S.R.A. as individual members. There has to be a governing body of any sport and Squash is no exception, so it should be the aim of all players to make that body truly representative of all the individuals and clubs that it is trying to serve, and financially able to carry out its desired tasks. The S.R.A. is a very democratic body, designed to make it easy for any member, club or individual to put up suggestions, comments or criticisms, and have them discussed at the highest level. The Council is the chief 'committee' and consists of representatives of all interested bodies in the country, plus the area representatives (the country being divided into six geographical areas of about seven counties each) and eight members, who are elected by the individual members of the S.R.A., with four retiring each year. The whole Council is too large and its members come from too far afield for it to meet regularly and actually run the sport directly, but one of its main functions is to elect a Management Committee to act as the executive committee for the year. Any major matters do, of course, have to be referred to the Council, but by and large, the Management Committee, aided by its numerous Sub-Committees, runs the game in this country. It meets, on an average, about every three weeks, and when it is remembered that all its members are also on at least one of the sub-committees and the Council as well, it can be seen that it is not exactly a sinecure to be elected to serve on this committee!

I said that the S.R.A. was a democratic body, but so far I have only mentioned the individual members' representa-

24

tives to show this. How does an ordinary player get his grouse or suggestion aired? The official links in the chain of communication are via the club secretary, who will raise the point with his county secretary, who will pass it on to the area representative. The latter can either get it put on the agenda of the next Council meeting and speak on it himself, or if that is too far in the future, he can ask the Secretary to raise it at the next Management Committee meeting. If the individual feels this is a long-drawn-out process and his idea is worthy of immediate attention he can ring the Secretary of the S.R.A. direct and by-pass 'middlemen', although of course the latter serve the very useful purpose of answering a lot of questions that have been asked before, giving reasons why such and such is, or is not, done and so on, thereby saving the Secretary and Management Committee from having to deal with the same points repeatedly.

I have always felt that Squash presents a challenge and a set of problems quite different from any other sport, and it is through intelligent discussion that the right answers will be reached. No doubt intending to be helpful, various people have from time to time gone to great lengths to tell me how other sports solve their problems, obviously considering that Squash can and should emulate these methods. Unfortunately, this is neither possible nor desirable; we have to worry out our own solutions. For instance, unlike the major team sports, and unlike Tennis, and even Table Tennis and Badminton, from among the racket games, Squash has no chance of ever getting much money out of spectators, and so has to keep its administrative costs within its limited means. In coaching, mass instruction just is not possible: unlike Tennis, when large numbers can practise by hitting the ball up against a wall, Squash practice is really only of any value when it takes place on a court, because of the need to use side walls as well as the front wall. In the chapter on coaching, I shall be mentioning a number of things which apply particularly to Squash, and in some instances, to no other game. If one merely copied the Tennis or Badminton coaching ideas, these points would be missed. Similarly, the development of the game has to come as a result of existing centres of Squash, like London, Birmingham, and the Tyne-Tees area, spreading, rather as certain plants in a flower bed gradually grow outwards, until the whole bed is filled, with only occasional help from the odd seed that springs up on its own in a new area. While this is happening, the areas into which the country is divided for administration and for inter-county competition, are not necessarily the areas generally accepted by other sports or organizing bodies as the logical subdivisions of the country. There is a great danger, I feel, that such excellent bodies as the Sports Council and the C.C.P.R., which do a tremendous amount of good in developing sport, may fail to see the individual problems and situations of the different sports they help to administer, and may try to steamroller and stereotype all sports into conveniently similar organizations, just because such systems have worked in games with which they are more familiar. As in coaching, so in organization and administration, I am rootedly averse to stereotypes and rigid forms. Of course I want 'discipline' and an ordered system, but a system in which individuals can use their talents, committees exercise their freedom of decision to bring about changes, and which is flexible enough to bend with the rapidly altering circumstances of a developing sport. This is where individuals must come in, and as I have said, the S.R.A. is a democratic body in which individuals can and should make their suggestions and criticisms heard. So do talk about the game, for your own enjoyment and entertainment, but if in the process something emerges from your discussions that could be of help or interest to the game generally, let us know at the S.R.A.

2: From Airshot to Achievement

For the beginner

So you want to play Squash. Well, first of all, you had better understand what the aim of the game is, and roughly how it is played, so that you can realize what you need to do and learn to become a good performer.

Perhaps it is easiest to imagine what Squash is all about if one starts with the more generally known game of Lawn Tennis. Here one has two players, each with a racket, playing a game with a ball. One serves to the other, and the rally continues until one of them fails to return the ball correctly, either by hitting it out of court, or into the net, or not hitting it before it has bounced twice. Squash is the same, except that where the Tennis net is, there is a high wall, and instead of one player hitting the ball over the net to his opponent, he now has to hit the ball on to this wall above the 'tin', the Squash equivalent of the net, and it then rebounds to his opponent, who has come round to the same side of the net, so to speak, and in turn has to return the ball over the tin. Just as in Tennis, the ball may not bounce before clearing the tin, but may be volleyed or allowed to bounce once after hitting the 'front' wall (i.e. crossing the net), but not twice. In addition to this front wall, there are walls along the 'tram lines' and the 'baseline', so that a Squash court is a four-walled room. The ball may hit any of these other walls on its way to or from the front wall, as long as it does not go 'out of court'. The legal part of the walls is denoted by a series of lines; across the top of the front wall, there is a line 15 feet from the ground, and another on the back wall 7 feet from the ground,

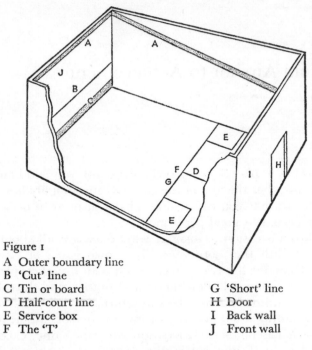

Figure 1
A Outer boundary line
B 'Cut' line
C Tin or board
D Half-court line
E Service box
F The 'T'

G 'Short' line
H Door
I Back wall
J Front wall

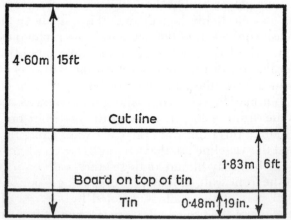

Out of court line

4·60m | 15ft

Cut line

1·83m | 6ft

Board on top of tin

Tin   0·48m | 19in.

FRONT WALL

Figure 2 (*above and right*). Dimensions of the Squash court.

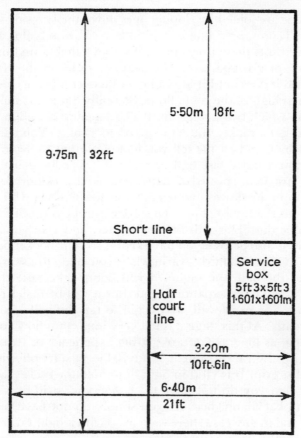

Short line

5·50m 18ft

9·75m 32ft

Service box
5ft 3 x 5ft 3
1·601 x 1·601 m

Half court line

3·20 m
10 ft 6 in

6·40 m
21 ft

FLOOR OF COURT

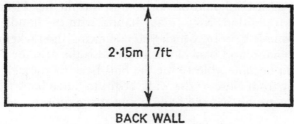

2·15m 7ft

BACK WALL

and these are joined by sloping lines down the two side walls. Unlike Tennis, on a line is 'out' in Squash, so a ball is out of court if it hits these lines, the walls above them, anything in the roof, or if it goes over any beam or rafter in the ceiling. Provided it does not hit anything, or go over a beam, the ball can go as high as the roof allows. So really Squash is simply a game in which two players hit the ball against a wall in turn.

Now, get a racket and let us go on to a court. You will also need a ball, and let me tell you first of all that to begin with you want a fairly fast ball to make it easier for you to hit. There are four speeds of ball, denoted by coloured dots, going from the slowest, which has a yellow dot, via white and red up to the fastest, blue. To start with, use one with a red or a blue dot. This will bounce higher, and give you more chance. It also helps if you have kept it in your pocket beforehand, so that it is fairly warm when you come to use it. The warmer the ball, the higher it will bounce, because the air inside it will have expanded, and thus it will be easier to hit. Go up to the front wall, and begin to tap the ball against it very gently. At this stage it is not very important how you are standing, as long as you are getting experience in striking a ball with the racket, but it is advisable to start off with an orthodox grip. It is vital in Squash to hold the racket in such a way that you do not have to change your grip from forehand to backhand, because you simply do not have time to do so, and in any case there is no need with a light racket and ball to move your hand at all.

Perhaps one of the easiest ways of describing how to grip the racket correctly is to tell you to hold the racket in the other hand, along the shaft, with the head away from you. The racket itself should be horizontal, but the head in an up and down position. Now 'shake hands' with the handle, find a comfortable grip by which you can swing the racket easily both forehand and backhand, and that is the grip for you.

As you become able to hit the ball back to yourself fairly regularly from close to the wall, begin to move back from it, until you are hitting the ball up and down quite consistently
30

from half or three-quarters of the way to the rear wall. Now check the position of your feet; initially you may have begun by facing the front wall. This was perfectly all right for what you were doing at that time, but now you must realize that frequently in an actual game, you will wish to use a wide range of shots, and play them in a variety of directions. This can only be done if you get into a position from which they are all possible, and ideally one should be facing the nearest side wall (whether forehand or backhand), and transferring your weight on to the front foot as you go through with the shot. This will enable you to be balanced as you play the stroke, and allow your wrist to produce whatever variety you want. So now return to your basic hitting up and down the court until you can do this regularly on both forehand and backhand, with your feet in the correct position, your grip not changing and your weight moving on to the leading foot as you play the ball.

It is vitally necessary early in your Squash life to realize that your opponent is going to be in the same area as yourself. In Tennis or Badminton, for example, it does not matter at all how widely you swing your racket. Your opponent is yards away and quite safe. In Squash he is close to you, and you often cannot see how close he is. Therefore you must develop a style that is safe, and is not going to fill the already overcrowded hospitals of the world, as you scythe your way through your opponents. The rules, of course, cover this point, but this is not much consolation to an opponent who has just lost an eye, any more than a feeling of righteous indignation is to a pedestrian who has been injured on a crossing. The main trouble is the follow-through; your opponent should leave you free to take a normal backswing, but after you have played your shot, you must let him get at the ball, and this he cannot do if you follow right round with your racket in a huge horizontal arc. It is quite unnecessary, as well as being highly dangerous, to do so. The racket should finish its swing, and lose its momentum in an upward direction, rather than continue on a scything course, and it is essential to make quite sure early on that you are not going to become a menace. Tennis players in particular, and ladies and young players whose wrists are not yet very strong, often try to get power into their shots by increasing backswing and follow-through, and have to be broken of the habit before they cause serious injury, so do please be careful.

One other early 'don't': make quite sure that you are not wearing black soled shoes when you go into a Squash court. These make black marks on the floor, which very quickly not only becomes unsightly in appearance, but also a dark and difficult background against which it is difficult to pick up the flight of a fast-moving ball. The rest of your clothing is immaterial at this stage, provided the decencies are observed, but when you start to play in matches, you will be expected to wear all white.

Let us now assume that you have got to the stage of hitting the ball fairly often, and you want to begin playing somebody else, and trying to beat them. In order to have a proper game, you will want to know the basic rules, how you score, what the various strokes are, and a few ways of practising them. So I shall start with the rules and the method of scoring.

A Squash match usually consists of the best of five games, and a game is won by the player who scores nine points first. You only score a point if you win a rally when you are actually serving, and if you win a rally when not serving, the score remains the same, but you take over the right to serve, and therefore to win points on subsequent rallies. While you are serving and winning rallies, you continue to serve from alternate sides of the court, but whenever you start a match, a new game or win the service during a game, you may elect to begin serving from whichever side you like. The service rule is a little complicated, and I will deal with that in a moment, but once the ball is in play the rally continues until one player wins it, as we have already said, because his opponent hits the ball into the tin or out of court, or fails to get it up before it bounces twice on the floor. The only additional point to remember about the scoring is that if the score reaches 'eight all', the person who is not serving at that moment elects either 'Set Two' or 'No Set'. If the former, the game continues until one player wins it 10–9 or 10–8; if the latter, it ceases at 9–8 to one or the other. In no case, can the game continue beyond 10.

Now the Service. The easiest way of remembering the rules about the Squash service is to keep in mind the number '3'. There are three basic requirements which are necessary for a correct service, three ways of serving a single fault, and three ways (unlike Tennis) of serving a double fault in the one stroke. First of all, the three things that are needed for a correct service. On each side of the court, on the floor, there are marked out little squares, known as the service boxes. A server must have at least one foot in the box, touching the floor at the moment he strikes the ball with the racket. The other foot may also be in the box, or anywhere outside it, or off the ground at the time, provided that the one foot which is inside the box is wholly within it, as far as the part which is in contact with the ground is concerned. That is to say, it is enough to have the tip of a toe on the floor, but not enough, if the whole foot is in the box with the heel just touching a line on the floor. The ball must then be thrown in the air and hit direct on to the front wall below the out-of-court line at the top, but above the 'cut' line, which is the one across the middle of the wall. I should remind you now, as you will perhaps have realized from the footfault rule, that the lines in Squash are 'out', unlike Tennis, and therefore in this case the ball must hit the front wall in the space between the two top lines. It must then rebound, so that it will land in the opposite back quarter of the court to that from which the service was delivered. Landing on the floor lines enclosing that quarter, or anywhere in the rest of the court makes the service a fault. So much for the three things necessary for a service to be 'good'.

The three types of single fault are as follows: a footfault, in which the server did not have his foot correctly grounded at the moment of striking the ball; a service in which the ball struck the front wall above the 'tin', but on or below the cut line; or a service which landed on the lines on the floor or outside the opposite back quarter of the court. Also a single fault is a service which combines two or all of these errors in the one service. As in Tennis, after serving a fault the server has another go, and if the second service is correct, the rally is on, but if it is not good, that is a double fault. Unlike Tennis, however, the receiver may accept the fault simply by playing a shot at it, and by doing so makes the service good. He is also allowed to volley the service, if he wishes, and of course in that case he makes it a correct service, even though it has not yet bounced in the required area.

Now for the three types of double fault; in this respect Squash is quite different from Tennis, as the rules adjudge some errors to be so heinous as to make the one stroke a double fault! The first is failure by the server to hit the ball at least above the tin on the front wall; this covers everything from a complete 'air shot', through one that lands on the floor, to the shot that just touches the top of the tin. The second is when the service goes 'out of court', i.e. is struck on to any of the four top lines on the walls or hits anything above them, just as in a rally; and the third occurs if the ball strikes any other wall on its way to the front wall. During a rally it is perfectly all right for the ball to go via a side wall, but the service must hit the front wall direct.

So much for the actual rules about the service, the rally and the scoring. Now I must tell you the best types of service and how to return them, the elementary 'tactics' of the game, and how to practise the various shots for use in a rally.

The ideal service is the 'lob' service. The object of this is to put your opponent under pressure by forcing him to play a ball which is coming off the side wall at an angle, dropping very steeply, and bouncing on the floor before it reaches the back wall, so that it will not rebound from it if left. Obviously, to do this, the ball must be hit high and wide, in order to get the steep drop and the angle off the wall, and

34

therefore the server should stand well forward in the serving box, and as close to the side wall as possible. This means, eventually, serving backhand from the backhand side of the court, though at first this may prove a little difficult. The further forward and the wider you can stand, the wider is the angle you can get on the front wall, which will calculably widen the angle on the back wall and make it less likely that the ball will rebound from it, if it does get that far; and the easier it is to hit the ball upwards on to the front wall, in order to get it to continue upwards, and then fall steeply, striking the side wall just below the out-of-court line, where the opponent will not be able to volley it. A really good lob service is worth a great deal; initially, your fellow beginners will often not return it at all, and even at the top level, where it will not be a winner, it will certainly often gain you the initiative. It is, therefore, well worth a lot of practice. After all, you are serving, and if you can win the rally, you will score a point, so it is very valuable to gain the initiative in the first stroke. But do remember one thing if you are practising on your own; it is no good standing around with a cold ball, solemnly hitting perfect services into the back corners, because as soon as you get into a game, the ball will warm up, and this wonderful shot of yours will go sailing into the roof now the ball is at match speed. So if you are going to practise on your own, make sure you keep the ball well and truly warmed up, while you are practising.

The best service is hit from underneath, and lobbed up on to the front wall. Now, there is no one magic spot on the wall to aim at; it depends on the speed of the particular ball, the height of the roof, your own height and way of playing the stroke and whether or not your opponent has a particularly good or bad shot at the service if it is higher or lower, coming at more or less of an angle off the side wall and so on. But basically the ball should hit the front wall about in the centre of the rectangle formed by the cut line and the out-of-court line with the side walls, and should be going upwards as it strikes the wall, so that it continues upwards, reaching its maximum height about a third of the way back down the court. It should then strike the side wall high up, partly to give the receiver a ball coming at an angle, partly to take pace off so that it will 'die' even more quickly at the back of the court, and it must bounce before reaching the back wall for the same reason. All this requires accuracy, practice, and the ability to adjust your shot with varying speeds of ball, heights of court roof and differing opponents, but it is well worth doing.

However, I know some players will rapidly point out that their home courts have very low ceilings, or dangling lights, or that they are so hot that the ball always rebounds violently and they keep serving double faults as their services rocket into the third row of the gallery. Also, of course, variety is always useful, and the second most useful service is the 'defensive' service, which is almost exactly the opposite in every way of the lob type. It is struck from as near the centre of the court as possible, it is hit safely above the cut line two-thirds of the way across the court with the aim of making it return reasonably close to the side wall. The idea is that even if this service will not be likely to gain the initiative for the server, it will be safe, will not run any risk of going out of court, and will at least restrict the return of service to a fairly defensive sort of shot. In addition to its value on a low-roofed court or with a fast ball, it is often a useful stroke at a vital stage in a game when the server must run absolutely no risk of hitting an ambitious lob service out of court.

These, then, are the two basic services; there are others, but they have merit only as very occasional surprise items; in themselves, they are inferior to the two we have discussed. The overhead Tennis type of service is useless; unlike Tennis, you canot belt the ball past your opponent, because the front wall takes most of the speed off it, and the harder it hits the back wall, the further it will rebound from it, and the easier the opponent's stroke will become. Sometimes it is useful, as a surprise, to hit the ball down the middle of the court, but this has a built-in snag, in that the server himself has to wait by his service box in order not to be hit by the return, and an alert receiver will either play a winner, or will at least force the server to sprint across to the other side of the court. There is also a service hit high on to the front wall, close to the server's own side wall, so that the ball rebounds on to the latter, and careers across court into the opposite back corner. Again, the surprise element may be of value, but an alert receiver will find himself dealing very comfortably with a ball approaching in the wide open spaces of mid-court.

Now, having shown you how to serve perfectly, so that no opponent can ever deal with the utterly brilliant stream of 'aces' flowing from your inspired racket, let us now switch to the receiver of the service, and show how no service need have any terrors at all if you do the right things.

First of all, where should you position yourself? Clearly, as the service has to come into the opposite back quarter of the court from where the server is standing, you should be somewhere in that area to receive it! You also know that the service is likely to be a high lob service or one close to the side wall, and obviously it is easier to move forwards than backwards. I, therefore, recommend that you stand in the rear corner of this quarter of the court, closest to the centre of the court, and prepare to move forward and towards the side wall as and when you see where the service is going. Now, if you can, imagine a triangle joining three points within the area that the server is aiming at, one just in front of you, one near the corner of the court and one just behind the service box. Two sides of the right-angled triangle are parallel to the back wall and the side wall, eighteen inches from them. An area is thus described, extended upwards of course, within which you can play the ball, while it is well clear of a wall. It is mathematically impossible to serve so that the ball 'dies' in the back corner without at some stage crossing this triangle, so it is up to you to gauge when it will do this, and so present you with a fairly comfortable stroke. It will either hit the side wall in front of your triangle and rebound into it, or will cross it before hitting the side wall, and in either case

37

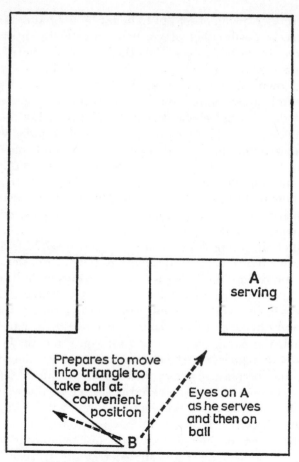

Figure 3. Preparing to receive service.

you have your moment to hit it, provided you have moved to the right place. The reason I suggest you stand right back to start with is to help you judge where the ball would hit the back wall, if you allowed it to do so. A ball which would hit this wall knee high or above should be allowed to do so, unless you have a good volley and choose to use it, because it will rebound well into the court and give you an easy shot. If you

38

estimate it will hit the back wall below knee high, or bounce first, then never let it get there! Of course, the 'triangle' is only needed to deal with the very good service; the piece of rubbish that arrives in the middle of the receiving area, well clear of the wall, can be dealt with summarily without recourse to Euclid! One other point: I said earlier that the receiver was allowed to take a single fault, if he so desired. Obviously there will be cases when he cannot reach the ball, or does not want to play it, but there are many occasions when in fact this fault presents him with a pretty easy return, and it is very much in his interests to play an attacking shot at it, rather than let it go and find that the server concentrates a good deal harder on the second service, and succeeds in setting some problems in the 'triangle'.

The basic return of service is a stroke down the nearest side wall, aiming to make the ball cause the opponent problems in the back corner of the court, and indeed this is always a sound shot at any stage in the rally, as well as when returning the service. A useful alternative is to hit the ball high over your opponent in the centre of the court, aiming to cause him embarrassment in the opposite rear corner of the court. If the service is a poor length and direction, then the receiver can select one from his vast, we hope, repertoire of winning strokes and dispose of the ball in whichever direction he thinks fit, but it is unwise to be too ambitious and attempt a winner from a good service, as if it does not come off, you have presented the server with a point, and he only needs nine of them to win the game.

One final point on receiving service: it is vital, as you stand at the rear corner of your triangle, poised to leap forward into it to frustrate the wiles of your opponent, that you give yourself the maximum chance of doing just that! You must give yourself the full time to make your calculation about where the ball will go, how fast it is likely to be coming and so on, by watching the server as he actually serves. Too many players watch the front wall, and so lose at least a third of the calculation time available to them, plus all the informa-

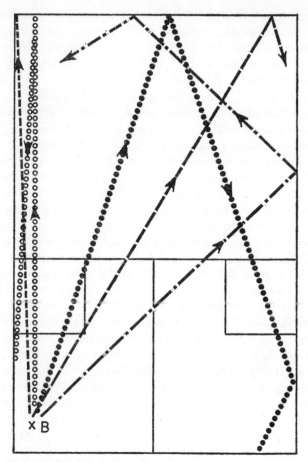

Figure 4. Possible returns of service.

1. ○○○○○○○ Drive or lob along side wall, to good length
2. ●●●●●●● Cross-court lob
3. ━ ━ ━ ━ ━ Straight drop shot
4. ━━ ━━ ━━ Cross-court drop
5. ━ ▪ ━ ▪ ▪ Reverse angle

1. and 2. defensive; 3., 4., 5 aggressive.

tion in advance of what sort of service it was from the actions of the gentleman purveying it! The front wall watchers may well be surprised by a hard hit service coming straight at them, or alternatively guess wrong about the flight of a good lob service, because they picked it up too late.

Now I want to suggest to you how you can practise the service and return. It is much better to do this with a friend, taking it in turns to act as server and receiver. I shall be saying later on that it is most desirable for practice games to be competitive, because this prevents practice from deteriorating into something boring and mechanical, and after all one is preparing for a highly competitive game. So with service, I always suggest that two players can best practise this by doing as follows: player A takes the role of server first, and player B the receiver. A has twenty services, and, exactly as in a proper match, has to serve from alternate sides of the court, and may select whatever type of service he wishes each time. B has to return the service as well as he can, attempting winners whenever he feels he can reasonably do so, and making sure the more difficult services are returned safely. A, then, has to play the third shot of the rally, and provided he does so correctly, the rally ends in a draw at that point. A scores a point every time B fails to return the service, either because it was too good for him, or because he went for an over-ambitious return and missed it. B scores a point when he retrieves the service in such a way that A cannot play the third shot of the rally. Thus, after A's twenty services, the score may be four 'aces' to A, three winning returns to B and thirteen draws. B will then have his twenty services and try to achieve a better result than A's four to three. Both players are thus fully practised in both roles, under proper competitive conditions, and the ball is kept at a proper match speed by the three-shot rallies.

So far, to help beginners follow more easily what I was saying, I have referred to the 'server' and the 'receiver'. In Squash, the correct term for the server is 'Hand-in' and for the receiver 'Hand-out'. A 'Hand' is a number of rallies in which the same player retains the service, and one might say that a player 'won the game in one hand', meaning that he had served right through it, winning nine consecutive rallies. You will hear the Marker, calling the score of a match, shout 'Hand-out two three' for example. This means that A had been serving at 'three two' but had lost the rally, and so became Hand-out, and B was just beginning his new Hand at 'two three'.

So far, we have launched the rally with our expert services and superb returns. What about the rally itself that follows on? We have to discuss two things, tactics, and the various strokes one may, and should, use.

There are two sorts of 'tactics' in Squash, to my way of thinking. Elementary and Advanced, or Match, tactics. The difference is that Elementary tactics are those which are always right, regardless of the type of court, the speed of the ball, the skill or shape of one's opponent or any other fact. Match tactics depend entirely on these variables, and what may be right and sensible for one opponent on one court, will be ludicrous on another court with a different opponent. I will go into these Match tactics in the next chapter, but the Elementary ones are important from the moment two beginners first start having rallies.

The first, and absolutely vital one, is to remember to move to the 'T' after every stroke, starting from the service. The 'T' is the position in the centre of the court where the lines join. The whole game revolves around this. For instance, it means that to move to the 'T' yourself, your opponent must have been moved away from it by your previous stroke, and furthermore, that previous stroke must not enable your opponent to play the ball between you and the 'T', thus preventing you from getting there. When you have arrived there, it is obvious that you are in the most central position in the court, and can retrieve anything your opponent can throw at you, and in addition, if he is foolish enough to return the ball to you while you are still there, then as you are in the centre of the court, he must be in one of the four quarters, and you have a very good chance of playing a winner into the corner of the court opposite to the quarter in which he finds himself.

I use the simile of the Oaktree! If you can imagine a large oaktree, sawn off about twelve feet high, planted in the centre of the court, this represents roughly the area which a player can cover with one foot on the 'T'. The radius of the oaktree is from the 'T' to just inside the serving boxes. Thus, every time a player strikes a ball against the front wall, so that it rebounds and hits the oaktree, he ought to have lost the point. It follows then, that players should aim to play their shots up and down the side walls, lob over the top of the oaktree, or play shots into the front corners. At all costs avoid bringing the ball back down the middle of the court.

So Tactic 1: get to the 'T' after every stroke, as fast as you can, and plant your oaktree; make sure your shots do not return into your opponent's oaktree, and acquire the range of shots you need to put the ball away, whenever your opponent is kind enough to hit yours!

The second tactic is one I always refer to as 'Blinkers'. So many players voluntarily limit their arc of vision, that is to say put on metaphoric blinkers like a horse, by gazing fixedly at the front wall. The problem is that in Squash, unlike most of the other racket games, your opponent is more often than not playing a shot from behind you, and in order to get any idea of how hard he is hitting it and to anticipate its direction, it is absolutely vital to follow the flight of the ball right on to his racket. Also, if you do not do this, you may well find that the ball has rebounded further from the side or back wall than you anticipated, and you are in considerable danger of being hit by your opponent! The 'blinkers' habit probably stems from Tennis, Table Tennis and Badminton, when you are watching a ball approaching you from in front, and an opponent playing his strokes more or less dead ahead of you, but in Squash, your opponent ought to be behind you, and it is vital to watch him play his shots all the time.

Thus Tactic 2: do not be a 'front wall watcher', but follow the ball round when it goes behind you to the back of the court, and see where and how hard your opponent is hitting it.

Perhaps it hardly counts as a 'tactic', but I think we should mention at this stage the need for speed and fitness in Squash. Quite obviously to return to the 'T' after every shot, and to be there and have the oaktree in position before the opponent can play his shot, means moving at considerable speed. It is useless planting your oaktree after the ball has gone through where it would have been, had you moved quicker! So speed back to the 'T' is every bit as important as speed to the ball, when it is your turn to play; and when you realize that in a close game of Squash, on a hot court, the rallies can last well over a hundred shots, you will appreciate that stamina is going to play its part too!

I have always steered clear of advising people on how to get fit, because I believe this is a very personal problem, and what may help one player may hinder another. For instance, most people do not like playing for a few hours after a heavy meal, but I have known some top players who insist on eating immediately before a match, and feel weak if they cannot do so. Others run round the block for hours every evening, while their opposites claim that this may indeed improve stamina, but reduces one's speed. Some people believe in weight training, others claim that this is a waste of time that should be spent playing Squash on court.

My own feelings are that it is up to each person to find out how he personally reacts to the various possibilities. After all, one player may naturally be very quick and agile, but lack stamina, whilst another may be able to run for ages, but at the speed of a veteran cabhorse, and needs to speed up. The first may need to go for long runs, and the second to buy a skipping rope! Certainly, I do believe that whatever other form of training one does, one must never cut down on time actually spent playing Squash on court, preferably competitively. You must never lose sight of the fact that your mind has to be working very quickly during a match, and must be co-ordinating the efforts of wrist, arm, leg, lung and everything else. Just running, or weight training, or skipping, may be fine in a very limited way, but they are only toning up a part of the forces under the command of the brain, and only by exercising the whole lot will you really improve your match play.

So point 3: do get fit, do move as fast as you can, both to the ball and back to the 'T', and do remember that the best practice for Squash is an actual game of Squash, played seriously and competitively.

My remark about the mind having to work quickly in a match brings me to the next point. If all one had to do was swipe the ball somewhere at the front wall each time, then the mind could happily switch over to 'automatic' and have a break. The work that the mind has to do is to select the correct shot each time. How you train it to do that is the subject of the next chapter, but what is important now is to explain what are the various strokes that the mind has to pick from, how they are played and how they can be practised.

Basically, there are eight different shots, which can be played from anywhere in the court, except when you are within a foot or two of a wall, when the latter inhibits the movements of your racket necessary to produce some of the shots. In reality, there are four types of shot, but these can each be hit to either side of the court. For example, there are the drop shots; the 'straight' drop is aimed to hit the front wall as close to the tin as is safe, and rebound to land in the 'nick'—the crack where the wall and floor join—close to the front wall, and to the side of the court nearest to where the player is standing as he plays it. The 'crosscourt' drop is played in the same way, but towards the side wall furthest from the player. Similarly with the angle shots; an 'angle' is a shot which hits a side wall before it hits the front wall. Usually one refers to an 'angle' shot or a 'straight angle' when the ball hits the side wall nearest to the player, and a 'reverse' angle when the ball is pulled across court to hit the further side wall first. The other two types of shot are the lobs or the hard hit strokes, which again can be played across court or down the side of the court nearest the striker.

It is now obvious that the range of shots is much wider than in other sports, and this variety must be used to deceive and wrong foot one's opponent, and to hit the ball into the furthest corner of the court from where he was last seen to be. If you can convince an opponent that you have all the shots at your command, he will be quite unable to guess where you are going to hit the ball next, but if you only produce a limited number of them, he finds anticipation much easier and has far fewer problems. On this question of anticipation, remember that it is important not to advertise one's shots by getting into any exaggerated or different positions to play them. I remember once beating an opponent by making frequent (and probably fortuitous) use of the reverse angle, a shot he simply never attempted. Clearly, the lesson went home, and he decided he had better develop a reverse angle too. Unfortunately, he could only play it by running round the ball and virtually playing a normal forehand drive across the court. This made his intention crystal clear to the opponent standing on the 'T', and the latter strolled up to the ball and played a winner into the wide open spaces. So it is important to approach every shot in exactly the same way, and to prepare for each with the same backswing. The variety comes from last-minute use of the wrist, not from changing position or swing. In top Golf, it seems to me, speaking as a genuine 84 handicap player, that the stars play all the shots very much the same way, and alter the length and height of the ball's trajectory by choosing the correct club. The Squash player's wrist has to do for him what the different club faces do for Palmer and Player. He does this in two ways; he has to change the angle of the face of the racket as it strikes the ball so that it either lifts the ball or hits it flat, and he has to manoeuvre his wrist, so that he can hit the ball in about a 90° arc, from 45° into the nearest side wall, round via any part of the front wall to the 45° angle necessary to

46

produce the reverse angle on the further side wall. If, however, he can do all these things from a correct basic stance, his opponent will have no clue what is coming, and in any case will find it difficult to see last-minute racket adjustments 'through' the striker's body as he faces the side wall, and has his back to the 'T'.

Now let us analyse the various strokes. Remember the basic position, either forehand or backhand, is facing the nearest side wall, with the racket 'cocked' high on the backswing by means of the wrist and not the whole arm, and as the stroke is played the weight is transferred on to the front foot. Do not, in your eagerness to get back to the 'T', begin swaying away from the ball before you have completed the stroke.

Having moved to the ball then, let us see how the drop shot is produced. As in all the strokes, the racket should be parallel with the floor, and not in an up and down position, which makes it very difficult to make correct use of the wrist. The drop shot should be played as the ball comes opposite the front foot, preferably not too close to the floor. The ball is then 'guided' to the appropriate part of the front wall, and the racket allowed to follow through normally, finishing again in an upwards movement in front of the player. The racket can only be parallel to the ground, especially when the ball is low, if the striker is prepared to bend his knees and get his body to the right height for the shot. Remember to play a proper stroke at the ball, with back swing and follow through; jabs, pushes and prods may be tempting when you only want a little drop shot, but they cannot be played accurately, and again using the Golf analogy, you never see a good player taking a jab with a No. 2 iron from 60 yards; he plays a proper swing with a No. 8 and lifts the ball correctly. The degree to which a Squash player needs to 'open' the face of the racket as he plays his drop shot depends on the height of the ball and the speed at which it is approaching.

Angle shots are normally used aggressively from the front of the court, and defensively from the back, although if the ball is in an easy position at the back, a fast surprise angle or reverse angle may well be a winner, especially against a front wall watcher with blinkers on, who has not given himself a chance of seeing which way it is going. In the front of the court, an angle is normally used to deceive the opponent, and can be an alternative to either the drop shot or a hard hit stroke. Thus, the 'tickle' angle, in which the ball is flicked gently round the walls, is a soft shot aimed to draw the opponent up in anticipation of a drop shot close to the wall, while the ball is actually fading away round the other side of the striker. The alternative to the hard drive must also look like a hard shot to prevent the opponent from correctly anticipating one which is going to end up near the front wall, and therefore the ball must genuinely be struck firmly into the wall, with the aim of getting it to die across court by the other side wall. This can be done either by the wrist, or by taking the ball early or late, and is usually a mixture of both.

From the back of the court, the defensive angle shot is normally called a 'boast', which I believe is an alternative for 'boost', and indicates that the ball is being 'boosted' up on to the side wall, so that it will carry to the front wall. It is often necessary to use the side wall in this way when you have been passed or lobbed, and the ball is in a difficult position near one of the back corners. It cannot be returned direct to the front wall, because the ball is too close to the back wall to allow the racket to get in between with enough leverage to hit the ball the full length of the court. So the player has to get into a position where he can take a full swing, and hit the ball high, hard and as far forward as possible on to the side wall, so that it will reach the front wall. To do this a player must face the opposite side of the court, and be well clear of the side wall nearest him, where the ball is, so that he can get maximum leverage, and not be 'tucked up' as he plays the shot. He must be prepared to bend down in order to be sure of getting under the ball, and take a full swing, remembering to flick the wrist at the moment of impact, so that the racket head 'overtakes' the arm movement, and gives that extra, often vital, little bit of power for the really difficult ball in the corner. The two most common faults in playing this shot are running into the actual corner and finding one cannot hit the ball through one's own knee or tummy, and in any case there is no room to swing the racket, and trying to over-hit and forgetting to flick the ball upwards and forwards on to the side wall. The really hard flat hit blasts into the side wall, and comes out to bounce about a third of the way to the front wall, while a gentler shot is floating upwards as a good return.

The lobs are remarkably similar in play and aim to the lob service. A well-produced lob will cause the opponent problems as it lands nearly vertically in the back corner, having successfully floated over the topmost branches of the opponent's 'oaktree'. It is more likely to be a winner when played across court, because it will hit the opposite side wall harder and thus lose more pace, and consequently 'die' nearer the back wall, but on a court with a low roof there is little margin of error if one is to miss the dangling lights and beams, and yet clear the 'oaktree'. On these courts a semi-lob, a sort of looped drive, as close to the nearest side wall as possible, is often safer, and can be most effective. I have always felt that the lob is the most under-used shot in Squash; played well, it can cause opponents to be digging the ball out of the back corners and setting up subsequent winners, and in a court where the overhead background or lighting are anything but perfect, it can produce anything from eye-strain to airshots. It is also the only way of recovering position, when forced to scrape up a good drop or angle in the front of the court. If you find yourself out of position, and stretching for the ball, never try to play a delicate winner; being off balance, you are running far too big a risk of hitting it down. Even more emphatically, do not try to blast your way out of trouble. Three things may happen, and one of them probably will; either you will slash the ball straight back at yourself and be unable to avoid being hit, which is both painful and unhelpful, or you can put the ball straight

D   49 back on to your opponent's racket in the 'oaktree', giving him the greater part of the court in which to play a winner, while you are still out of position, or you can hit it narrowly past yourself, so that your opponent can, if he so wishes, drill you with the ball, which is as unhelpful to you and even more painful than the first possibility. So, if in trouble, give yourself time to recover position, and you can only do this by giving the ball height, so that your opponent cannot play his shot until it comes down within reach again, by which time you are back on the 'T'.

The vital thing about playing the lob is to get right under the ball. Just as a boast from the back wall is not dependent on power, but on an upwards and forwards 'flick', so the lob does not carry to the back corner by being hit hard, but by being hoisted upwards on to the wall. The harder a lob is hit, the further it will rebound from the back wall, and the lower its flight will be, thus making it more likely to strike the 'oaktree', or if its trajectory is right and it is still hit too hard, the more likely it will be to fly out of court.

It is much more difficult to be specific about the hard hit strokes. This is partly because players' natural ability affects the situation, as some people can naturally hit harder than others, whilst everyone can shove a lob up into the air, partly because the way and aim of hitting hard shots vary tremendously with the ball, the opponent and other factors like the score and the temperature of the court. Basically, there are three main aims behind the hard stroke. A player can be attempting a 'kill'; this means that he is trying to hit a winning shot in the front half of the court, and will usually aim at the 'nick' to give him an added chance of achieving this, either across court or into his nearest side wall. He can be attempting a drive to a good length, with roughly the same aim as the lobs, which is to embarrass his opponent in the back corners of the court. This is a much more effective stroke when played parallel to the nearest side wall, as it may 'cling' to the side wall, but also the cross-court drive will either run the risk of entering the opponent's 'oaktree' on its way to the opposite corner, or will hit the opposite side wall by the service box, which will certainly pull the opponent from his 'oaktree', but the ball will never finish up in the corner. Thirdly, the hard shot is used nowadays to set a fast pace to a game, without worrying too much about accuracy. The theory seems to be that if you swipe the ball hard enough and often enough, you will get it warm enough for the opponent to be unlikely to be able to play any 'touch' or soft winning shots, and by continually rushing him, force him into errors. To maintain this, you yourself have to be remarkably fit, and continually prepared to take the ball early, which is extremely tiring. The answer to this type of play is to lob continuously; I have always enjoyed seeing a 'rusher' frantically stamping up and down waiting for a lob to come within his reach, so he can have another go, whilst his opponent refuses to be stampeded, but this style of play, when done as well and accurately as by the Khans, or at Amateur Championship level by Mike Oddy, is most effective and tiring to play against after a while; for one thing the noise begins to get one down!

So much for the various shots; now I must suggest ways in which you may practise. Some people are able to set themselves targets for individual practice, and some are not! If I tell myself that I must hit fifty consecutive backhands or something, not only do I cheat, but usually when I miss one, convince myself that I was not ready! No doubt if you are one of the people who can spend hours on court on your own, you can improve the shots very considerably, but many of us become extremely bored extremely quickly, and when that happens, practice must come to an end! All one can practise alone is accuracy; it is impossible to create match situations, because in a match an opponent is plugging the ball at you in the way that it seems to him will be most uncomfortable for you, whereas when you have hit the previous shot yourself, you have some pretty good idea where it is going to finish up. You can, of course, do a spot of training, by playing for so many minutes flat out, regardless of which bounce you take the ball on, but if you keep this up for long, not only will anyone appearing in the gallery assume you are mad, which does not matter unduly, but you will probably drive yourself into an early grave, which does! My own feelings are that practice is much more enjoyable, and therefore useful, when done in pairs, and preferably when made competitive. After all, a match is competitive, and you are practising in order to play better in matches, so it seems logical to me that practice should also be competitive. Once you can play any stroke reasonably correctly, the next thing is to play it while moving about a court with someone else hitting the ball at you, and this is what practice in pairs is all about.

I have already given you a way of practising your service and return of service. Let us now assume that A and B want to practise the other shots. Remember that in all practices, it is vital that both players change roles half-way through, so that both get a fair shair of the various things being exercised, and that where applicable, the practice is done on both forehand and backhand. Let us first of all put A on the 'T' and instruct him to move up to the front forehand corner and practise lobbing into the back backhand corner. B, also beginning from the Oaktree area, must go into this corner and return the lob by means of a 'boast' shot, which will of course return the ball to the front corner for A to repeat his lob, and so on. Frequently B will not be forced to play a boast, but he should do so each time, just to get the 'feel' of the shot, and in fact, because he is playing it to rather easier balls than usual, it will succeed more than usual, and add to the confidence that the practice is giving him. The vital thing for both players is that between each shot they must return to the 'T'. In a match, they are never going to be allowed to stand in a corner and have the ball kindly presented to them, so the whole value of the practice lies in moving from the 'T', where they will be in a match, and playing the ball after moving into the correct position for doing so. One can 'spice' the practice a bit by suggesting to them that if A suspects that B is not returning to the 'T'

52

properly, he can slip in the occasional drop shot; if B gets to it, then he must have been doing the right thing, but if not, A has made his point. Similarly, B can throw in the occasional drive down the wall instead of his boast, and if A has not been coming all the way back, and incidentally has also not been watching behind him, then he will not get to it!

After a while, and after changing roles, and then practising backhand lobs and forehand boasts, we can revert to A in the front being told to practise drives down the walls to a good length. With B continuing to boast, A will now drive from alternate sides, as the boasts move the ball from one front corner to the other in turn. The next move is to tell B to practise drop shots from the back of the court, when not forced to boast by A's good length strokes. Eventually, you can have A lobbing across court or driving down the walls, as he likes, and B boasting or dropping, as he chooses. In all these little games, one can create ways of scoring, which add to the fun of the thing.

Now A and B want to have a go at angles. To far too many Squash players, the walls are simply there to hold the roof up, and they miss out on what to me is one of the great attractions of Squash. This is the wide range of shots at one's disposal, and the use one can make of the side walls for the angle shots. It is understandable that it does not come naturally to Tennis players to hit the ball deliberately into the 'tramlines' and 'side netting', so to speak, and the next game is designed specifically for them. A and B are put in the front half of the court and told to play a game consisting of rallies in which every shot is an angle or a reverse angle. In other words, every shot must hit a side wall on its way to the front wall. There are three benefits from this; primarily, each player improves his own production of the angle strokes, and because he is forced to play them all the time during this practice, they become something he actually thinks about and produces, and will therefore be more likely to think about and produce during his next proper match. Secondly, because his opponent is also doing nothing but produce angles, he gets a pretty concentrated look at a fellow playing these particular shots, and will therefore be more likely to anticipate them, when his next opponent plays a few at him. Finally, to have two players circling around in half the usual space is a very good exercise in keeping out of each other's way.

This 'front-half-of-the-court' game can also be adopted to practise the drop shot. It is obvious, if you think about it, that both players cannot play drops at the same time; they if try, after two or three shots, both are in the same corner in an embarrassing, if not actually illegal, position! The mixture of one playing angles, which move the ball out into the open court again, while the other tries his drops, is the best way of practising these.

One of the main difficulties of Squash practices in pairs is that you very seldom get an A and B of the same standard of play. This does not matter too much for the little exercises I have suggested to you so far, but when one gets on to the stage of practice games, it is only too easy to have a situation where one player is murdering the other, in such a way that it is no practice for him, and downright depressing for the other. I have found a couple of useful 'handicap' situations, which means that players of very different levels can both play flat out, with neither getting over-confident or unduly hopeless. The first is where the stronger player needs to win games as against his partner's points. Thus, if after four normal games, he is leading 9–0, 9–0, 9–1, 9–2, he is actually 4–3 up! It means that the stronger player must always go hard, even when 8–0 up, and because he is playing a weaker player, can afford to try out some shots he wants to practise, whilst the lesser brother need never be despondent even at 0–8, and will obviously improve his own game by playing someone much better. The other game is one in which the stronger player only scores when one of his services is not returned. If it is, the rally continues normally, and if he wins it, he continues to serve, from the other box of course, but the score remains the same. This means that the better player is

54

really having to concentrate on his service, as this is his only chance of scoring, and dare not let his opponent in, just in case he flukes a point, and so has to play the rallies flat out, whilst the opponent very quickly learns how to return even these excellent services to avoid losing points, and again has every incentive in the rallies, and will find his standard of play being improved by this practice against a superior player.

When talking about the shots, I stressed how important it was to use the full variety of strokes that Squash offers. It probably ought not to be necessary to add that this variety includes frequent changes of pace in the rallies, and yet one continually sees, and plays, people who play on a 'monotone'. They have some variety of stroke, but the drives and angles are all hit at the same speed, which is the same as the service, and the lobs and drops are not much slower. Even in a long rally, or perhaps I should say especially in a long rally, a sudden change of pace can upset an opponent; after a dozen hard drives, a gentle lob, or a volley drop, or a reverse angle from the back of the court, can all, by their very surprise value, cause a mishit, or break up an opponent's rhythm. If 100 represents the hardest drive ever produced, and 0 the softest drop, try to widen your range to as near 0 to 100 as you can. So many club players are content to live in the 45–70 range, and their games are very easily forecastable, and simple to break up and defeat.

I hope now I have given you some ideas for practice, explained what the shots are, and above all why you need them to win at Squash. In the next chapter, I hope to give advice to that most important part of a Squash player, his mind. Once you are fit and fast, have a good service and a safe return of service, and can play all the shots, you are halfway towards becoming a player. Now we must find out how best to use all the knowledge you have gained so far.

3: Mind over Matter

For the club player

If I ever get round to writing a book of verse about Squash, I shall write an ode to a veteran, which will run something like this:

> *They say that in Squash it is all in the mind,*
> *A question of mind over matter—*
> *In my case the matter is tum and behind,*
> *And the problem is mind over fatter!*

But joking apart, before middle-aged spread sets in, or some other physical handicap, and players can all get really fit, the one who wins is the chap who thinks about the game and trains his mind to produce the right answers at the right moments. And one must realize that an answer is required every time a shot is played. We have agreed in the last chapter that, on most occasions, eight shots present themselves for selection. If the ball is close to a wall, this number is reduced, but in any case, one would then be thinking of a safe return, because the situation would be a little dangerous, and the choice would be limited to one or two anyway. What we have to do now is discuss how to train the mind to select the best shot for each occasion.

What I want to suggest is that all Squash players should become computers! To me, the most completely un-mechanically minded person of all time, a computer is a machine into which you feed information, and at a given moment, you press a button, and after an appropriate interval for flashing lights and internal whirrings, out comes a card with the information you want. Obviously the thing works better if it is fed as much information as possible, and the information is accurate. The same applies to the computerized mind that I want all Squash players to develop. For example, a player may have a very good lob normally, and may go up to a ball, which normally he would consider right for lobbing; on this occasion, however, he happens to be in a court with a particularly low roof, and unless he has fed this piece of information into the computer, and the machine has correctly produced another answer, he will just carry on and hit the ball straight into the roof.

I suggest that you should begin feeding information into the computer before the match even starts, and continue to acquaint it of all the varying factors as the match goes on. The relevant facts that the computer must have in order to produce the right answer every time you press the button before each shot, concern the court, the opponent, the ball and one's own fitness before the match, and then as you go along, changing facts about your own and your opponent's state of fatigue, any alteration in the court, such as condensation developing, the score, whether Hand-in or Hand-out, which of one's own strokes are working well that day and so on.

Let us look at some of these points in more detail. First of all the court itself. If it is a court on which you have not played before, go and have a very good look at it before you even go and change. The important things to note concern the height of the roof, the 'background' overhead, the colour of the floor and tin, the position of the door, the possibility of condensation and any unusual or 'putting off' features, such as bad cracks or broken plaster, uneven or split floorboards, glass walls or panels, protruding ledges, galleries, ventilators or boards, and perhaps, if a game is actually in progress, you can get an idea of the acoustics! Obviously if the court has a low roof, with lights or beams that are hanging dangerously near where a good lob would need to go, then the computer must be instructed not to order lobs or lob services, but if the roof is high and there are no dangling lights, then of course

57

lobs are an excellent idea. The actual type of roof is important as well as the height; sometimes, as in the Bruce court of the Lansdowne, there is a clear well-lit background of diffused light, which is excellent for seeing the approach of a high shot. Other courts, some for instance built in old Rackets courts, with very high ceilings, and lights strung across on wires, offer a black background with six brilliant points of light, and it is virtually impossible to see a shot which is hit high enough and disappears into the Stygian gloom. Similarly, courts with 'fussy' ceilings, which have lots of beams and struts, glass panels, wires and metal handles, provide a very poor background against which to see a small black Squash ball. If, therefore, the ceiling is high, and is a poor background for a moving ball, then the computer will order more lobs than usual. In the same way, the colour of the floor can make a difference. The ideal background for a hard low shot is a clean, matched white maple floor, with a light painted 'tin' on the front wall. Often on old courts, or school courts, where the boys play in shoes which have been used for cross-country running and the like, the floors are very dirty indeed, and frequently even fairly new courts have very ill-matching floor boards, so that the ball is seen travelling over a maze of lines, like a train crossing the points at Clapham Junction. Again, the computer should be fed the information, in order to weigh up the merits of the hard low drive, and see if any advantage can be gained by playing more than usual.

Usually the court door is in the centre of the back wall, but this is not always so. There are courts where it is in the side wall, such as at the West London Club or the Royal Marines courts at Eastney, or at one end of the back wall, as in some of the courts at the Northwood Squash Centre. This is worth noting, because a door is never quite as solid as a wall, and if you are in the habit of using that particular part of the wall, where the door now is, for perhaps an angle shot, you may have to adjust your shot a little. Also, with wear and tear, the door frame, handle, the plaster round the frame and any bits and pieces may well become worn, or broken, and there will be the risk of bad bounces off the door, when the ball hits it.

The effect of condensation on the walls completely changes a game, and one has to alter one's tactics completely, if there are signs of moisture on the walls. This is not a problem on a well-heated court, or one in the centre of a large building, but it is a great nuisance on courts with outside walls, and no central heating. The danger comes when there has been a long frosty spell and the walls are very cold; all at once the weather changes and a warm, humid airstream suddenly meets the still cold, smooth surface of the walls, and just as the steam from a bath settles on the mirror or tiles in the bathroom, so this air deposits its moisture on the court walls. The effect is to make a ball skid along the surface, rather than rebound at the normal angle. As a result, it is impossible to attempt lobs, either on service or during a rally, because as the ball strikes the front wall, it shoots straight upwards into the roof. Angles, too, are useless, because they slide along the side wall, hit the front and return into the centre of the opponent's 'oaktree', instead of going correctly across court. Furthermore, the ball will collect a certain amount of moisture, and will tend to skid through on the floor, which makes any attempt to play a delicate drop shot rather a hazardous pastime. All one can do is to hit the ball hard and often, and as low as possible, preferably across court in the hope that it will surprise the opponent, as it skids down the wall past him. The only possible variation is the stop volley; the ball cannot misbehave in mid-air, so it is safe to attempt a winner up at the front of the court; after belting everything else to the back, you may well surprise your opponent. Anyway, when you look at your court, see if you can feel any moisture, and just consider whether conditions are such that condensation could occur later on, when a bit of warm human humidity starts floating around in the court.

It is often a good idea to make mental notes of any ugly plaster 'scars' or actual unevenness in the wall surfaces, so

59

that you will be expecting the occasional odd bounce and not be put off by it. Similarly, note any glass panels or walls, and anything overhanging the court which could trap an unwary lob. There are, for instance, courts with high ceilings which invite lobs, but the out-of-court lines are boards nailed on to the walls, and jutting out from them, instead of the recessed concave metal strip which is officially recommended.

So much for the court; note these points, store them away in the computer, and check them again when you actually go on court for the match. Now let us consider your opponent. If you have played him before, dig into the memory banks and see what happened then; what were his strong or weak points, and what conclusions did you come to about how to deal with him next time? It may be that he has improved or deteriorated since your last meeting, but until you find out differently, this is where you must start in your planning as far as he is concerned. If however you have never played him or seen him play, and therefore have no personal first-hand knowledge of him, you must find out all you can. Obviously, in a team match, some of your side may be able to help you, and this can be valuable information, even if it cannot be relied on completely. I am not suggesting that your friend is feeding you incorrect information, but not infrequently in Squash odd clashes of styles occur, and a player he found easy or hard to beat may prove the reverse to you, but at least, knowing your friend's type of game, you can gauge your opponent's ability up to a point.

You must place no reliability on opposition propaganda, and certainly none on anything your opponent says about himself! All such statements are, to a lesser or greater extent, intended either to frighten you and put you off, or else to lure you into a sense of false security. All remarks beginning, 'As I said when they asked me to play Number One for the County last week . . .' or 'I'm afraid I shall not be able to give you much of a game with this fractured fibula of mine . . .' should be received with the gravest suspicion. The first bloke is probably a rabbit, who was asked to play in a

County missionary side of old-age pensioners against a Prep school, and the other chap is probably related to H. Khan and has had no fibula trouble for twelve years. On some club notice boards, however, or in the various Squash publications that may be around the club, you may see some of your opponent's previous results, and be able to see some pattern in them. Maybe he always beats people you know to be hard hitters, and loses to the lob and drop experts, or vice versa. In any case, you may be able to get some clue about how to plan your game against him.

The last two things to feed into your computer before the match are details of the ball and your own fitness. The type of ball used at this particular club or in the competition in which you are playing, will be known in advance, and it is a factor, especially when the temperature of the particular day is taken into consideration. For instance, a 'yellow dot' ball ordered for a tournament in Edinburgh on a typical February day could behave a little differently from a White dot at the Junior Carlton club, where I reckon if you took an egg and a couple of rashers on court with you, you could have breakfast after the knock-up.

Your own fitness is a very important factor. If you are really fit, you will not be afraid of a long match, and will not want to play any risky shots early on for fear of losing the rally, when you ought to be fit enough to win it more safely later on. If you are suffering from a bad cold or some strain, on the other hand, you may well decide that you have simply got to go for winners before you run out of steam. If they come off, you may win; if they go wrong, you will lose, but if you do not even try them, you will lose anyway because of your illness or injury.

Now the computer has been prepared as far as possible before the actual moment when you walk on the court, but there are five more very important minutes yet for adding to the information you have already fed into it. I refer to the knock-up. Far too many players simply stand and swipe the ball around a few times rather aimlessly, and completely waste this valuable chance of acquiring information, practising strokes and generally doing all one can to be fully prepared for the first rally of the match. After all, there is a lot to do. First of all, check that what you suspected about the court is in fact true now you are on it. Is the roof really rather a poor background for sighting the ball? Is the wall beginning to sweat? And so check your previous ideas and amend the computer's data if necessary. Have a good look at your opponent. Is he getting on a bit, and therefore liable to be cunning and experienced, but a bit short on speed and stamina, or is he young, fast, fit, and so probably not blessed with a wide range of shots, but good at retrieving, and able to stand a long match. Is he very tall, and so difficult to lob, but vulnerable when made to turn and change direction, or short, and so easy to lob, but probably able to dart very quickly round the court. Watch his shots, and see what he seems to be practising most, and what he appears to play well. If you do all this, you can then start thinking about the ball, which ought to have warmed up to its match speed by then. You found out before what type of ball it was, but even balls of allegedly the same speed vary very considerably, and you have to discover how each one will behave at the temperature in the court that you are using. See how your own shots seem to be going, and which are working well on that particular occasion. It is not easy to forecast from one day to the next exactly which shots will be producing winners and which will be drilling the tin every time, so see which are successful in the knock-up, and this will give you confidence to play them when the match starts, and if you are confident, then they are that much more likely to be successful. In the same way, try to spot faults in your opponent, as well as any particularly effective shot, which you will obviously not give him many opportunities to play. If, for instance, you put up a couple of high lobs and he mishits them both, refrain from giving him any more during the knock-up, but leave him with the memory of two bad shots; then when the match starts in earnest, start lobbing at once in the hope that he will lack confidence in the shot, and continue to mishit. Conversely, if he has confidently disposed of your two lobs by belting them straight into a nick somewhere, you will refrain from presenting him with opportunities to continue to do so at your expense during the first game.

One other point about the knock-up is your basic position and movement during it. Only too often you see club players standing well back in the court, virtually motionless, swiping the ball to and fro to each other. It is important to move around yourself and become loose and warmed up, by taking some shots from the front and some from the back of the court. What is even more important is to get your eyes used to match conditions. When the game actually starts, you will aim to station yourself on the 'T', or a little behind it, but certainly not four feet from the back wall. So make certain during the knock-up that you are well up the court for most of the time, in order that your eyes may get used to the ball approaching from a front wall which is the same distance away as it will be in the match.

Now the knock-up is over, the sweaters are off and the chips are down. The computer has been stocked with all the data you can find, and you are ready to start pushing its button every time you go up to the ball and have to decide which shot to select. Assuming it tells you correctly, and assuming you are able to play the chosen shot well enough, and assuming you are fit enough to get your computer to the ball each time, I fail to see how you can lose! If you do, and it comes to all of us, you must analyse what went wrong. Did the computer do a good job of selecting the shots, but did you play them badly? Did the computer find itself selecting shots which appeared to be countered easily by the enemy, even though played well? Did the legs and lungs responsible for carting the computer around just fail to do so fast or often enough for the computer to win on its own? Do not expect the computer to produce a winning shot each time, because it has the overall aim of winning the match, and for a long time it may be selecting safe shots as the best ones to play at

63

that moment, because first of all it wants to take toll of a less fit opponent's stamina. Sometimes, if you are scraping a ball up in the front corner, it may come out with some purely desperate message on its card, such as, 'Hit it up in the air somewhere, and let's get the hell out of here.' It will always blend aggression with security as far as possible. Unless circumstances, such as rapid failure of owner's stamina, dictate otherwise, it will select the safe shot, which will keep the opponent under pressure, rather than the shot which may produce a winner but which is highly risky.

There are two other important considerations which the computer must be told to bear in mind. At the start of each game, there is a danger period when mishits can occur rather more frequently than when the game is fully in progress. This is for a number of reasons; nerves start to play a part, when the match is getting under way; sometimes players attempt shots which they have not revealed in the knock-up, and therefore have not practised, and so do not hit cleanly, and if they do, the opponent may be surprised and miss the ball; the ball may have cooled off at the end of the knock-up while the players were removing sweaters and spinning for service, and it will certainly change its speed if left on the court for the interval between games; and now for the first time, at the start of the match, the players are actually moving round the court, and in their initial eagerness may well obstruct each other slightly. Do try to counteract this by ordering the computer to be a little cautious in the first few rallies of a match. If there are going to be nervous mistakes, let it be the other chap who makes them, while you quietly and safely shovel the ball down the walls into the back corner. If you can get a lead of about 4–0 or 5–1, you can then start attempting your full range of flowing winners. If they go wrong, you can stop trying them while you are still ahead, and if they work, you find yourself a game to the good. At least you have a little fat to work on, and you will find that Squash is very like gambling. It is usually the tycoon, who could not care less if he wins or loses at the casino, who goes off with the jackpot, while the poor wretched schoolmaster, who really needs the cash, sees his monthly pittance disappear into the tycoon's pocket. It is wonderful what a little confidence will do, and alarming how anxiety can affect one's play. When you are 5–1, you play your drop shot confidently and in a relaxed way, and as a result, it is placed well and is a winner; you attempt the same shot at 1–5 down, and being over-anxious to get back into the game, play it rather nervously and down it goes. So do try to get your lead of a few points in every game.

The second thing to remember is that in Squash you are either Hand-in or Hand-out. It is stating the obvious to say that if you are Hand-in, you are in a position to win a point, and if Hand-out, you are liable to lose one. What I am trying to stress is that it is a little more sensible to take risks to play winners when you are Hand-in than when you are Hand-out. If they come off, when Hand-in, you actually score a point, and if they go wrong, you only lose the service, and the score remains the same. When you are Hand-out, however, you take the risk of actually losing a point, perhaps rather more of a risk because you have more need to win the rally, and may be nervous, and even if it comes off, you do not score a point, but just win the service, whereas if you miss it, you present your opponent with one-ninth of a game!

And so the game continues. The information should be brought up to date all the time, as your own stamina changes, if a new ball has to be produced, if your racket breaks, as the opponent seems to tire, as the court begins to sweat and so on. Major overhauls of computer information and larger questions for it to answer, can be done during the interval between games. But never turn the computer off; it should be working all the time, so sharply that it can assimilate, before providing its answer, the very last piece of information, such as any sound revealing the movement of one's opponent, and this should enable a really well-trained computer to switch from 'drop' to 'angle' in time.

Remember too to instruct your computer to vary its

answers according to whether the court is hot or cold. Tactics should vary considerably with the conditions. On a cold court, in mid-winter, it is well worth attempting lob, drop and angle winners, because if the shot is played well, it is so much more likely to be a winner, which justifies taking the risk. On a hot court the same shot, even if played perfectly, will not be a winner because the ball bounces much further and higher, and the opponent can reach it easily, and so the risk is not justified. Furthermore, on a hot court, the actual shot has to be played higher from the floor, normally with the ball travelling faster, and it is much less easy to play an accurate shot anyway. One has therefore to resign oneself to long rallies, and although one should still use angles, drops and lobs to move an opponent round the court, they should be played safely, and well above the tin, with no risks taken. The aim is to tire the other player by moving him around the court more than he can move you, and only attempt a winner if he has been manoeuvred right out of position. On a really hot court, a drop shot, even if hit very softly, will rebound a long way back down the court, and in order to draw the opponent as far up the court as possible, it is advisable to use angles and reverse angles, as these slide across the front wall, and do not come out as far as a much softer shot hitting it from directly in front.

These, then, are the things to tell your computer, the limits and orders to give it, and how to use it. Squash is an intelligent game, and I once heard it described as chess played fast. Only experience will make your computer work really efficiently, and train it to snap out its answers fast enough for you to translate them into winning shots.

4: 'Do As I Say, Not As I Do'

For the coach

Rather longer ago than I care to remember, I spent a year, after fooling the examiners and obtaining a degree, in taking the Diploma of Education. During this year, I was put in possession of more information, which at the time seemed of doubtful value, than at any other period in my life. However, I suppose some of it stuck and began to make more sense later. For instance, do you realize that the human race divides into three groups, the Visile, the Aurile and the Tactile? In other words, people may learn new things in one of three ways, by seeing them done, by hearing them explained or by actually doing them. Of course, there are the awkward customers who need to see it done, have it explained and be made to do it, and still get it wrong, but basically the point is that anyone instructing a person or a group, in a practical thing like Squash especially, must remember that his pupil may be in any of the three categories, and in any class he may have, there will certainly be representatives of all three, so that the coach must be quite certain to cover each piece of instruction in all three ways. If he wishes to teach a particular shot, he must show how it is done by a good demonstration, explain the mechanics of it clearly, and then make the pupil do it himself under supervision.

What I propose to do in this chapter is to give you some general hints on coaching and teaching which are relevant to Squash, but are also true of any subject, and then go on to some specific hints which apply purely to Squash coaching.

First of all, it is absolutely vital to make your instruction

67

interesting and enjoyable. However wholesome and filling it is, a steady diet of suet pudding gets a bit wearing after a time, and one would soon stop having lunch at a restaurant that never did anything more exciting than that! If you want your pupils to come back for more, they must be made to enjoy the time they spend in your charge. They must find it fun, have confidence in you, and feel that they are improving. I would far sooner leave a coaching session feeling that my pupils have really enjoyed it and will be back for more, than stuff them full of dull theory in a two-hour lecture, or set them half an hour of backhand shots up and down the wall, even if I could have done them more immediate good in one of the latter ways. If you think about virtually all the points I am going to mention in this chapter, I think you will see that they all lead back to these basic truths of the need for enjoyment, confidence in the coach, and a feeling of improvement.

One very important thing to remember is that you are an individual yourself, and every pupil you ever try to help will be an individual, too. By an 'individual', I mean that everyone has different talents, or similar talents in differing quantities. Two exactly equal players may have reached that standard by very different routes; one may have great natural talent, but no great ability to concentrate, and so plays a mixture of brilliant winners and quite horrible mishits, while the other chap has no outstanding flair for the game, but terrific determination, and he seldom hits a winner, but never makes an unforced error. Most players have a natural ability to play a particular shot particularly well, and quite often, play it in a somewhat unorthodox way. A coach must be prepared and able to spot his pupil's latent ability, and encourage any especially good shot the pupil may produce fairly consistently, even if he does not play it quite 'according to the book', while at the same time discouraging any shot which is clearly more dangerous than profitable in the long run. Furthermore, as the coach is also a person with his own abilities, weaknesses, and peculiarities, he must do things his
68

own way, within the overall correct umbrella of sound Squash coaching. He must never become stereotyped. In some sports, coaches are far too rigid; they turn themselves into sausage machines, turning out lots and lots of little sausages, all looking, smelling, and tasting alike. Any original bit of meat that had a slightly unusual shape, had all the edges knocked off on its way through the machine, and any chance it had of being a little different, a little better and bigger than its fellows, was lost. When one thinks of the great players of any sport, one can picture them 'doing their own thing', and doing it superbly. Are, or were, people like Denis Compton, Lee Trevino, Rocky Marciano, Pancho Gonzales, Barry John and, yes, Hashim Khan, merely super versions of the orthodox? Or, as I believe, great natural talents allowed to blossom to the full flower of their individual genius? Do, as a coach, make quite sure that you do not stunt the growth of any outstandingly promising beginner by putting him into a conformist strait-jacket. When I say a coach must do things his own way, I am not advocating a kind of anarchy in coaching; I want the right messages put across in the individual style of the coach. Just as within a Church, each minister is trying to put across the same message, but may do so in a flamboyant or a persuasive, a philosophical or a semi-humorous way, according to his own personality. So in any subject, each instructor must know his subject thoroughly, and then put it across in the way that suits him best. Never try to imitate someone else's methods, unless you are quite sure they will suit you, however illustrious they may be in their own field.

Another very vital point to remember is to avoid boredom. Never make a pupil do any one thing for too long, whatever it is. Too many instructors talk too much and at too great length. Not only to fit in with the idea of 'visile, aurile and tactile', but also to avoid boredom, break up your instruction with demonstrations, films, games, discussions, competitions —anything to maintain and inspire interest.

Remember, too, that it is a great spur to future effort if a pupil feels that he or she is making progress. To do his job properly a coach must be basically a critic; if he can find nothing to improve in the pupil, he is out of work! Luckily, perhaps, for those of us who teach, one can always find something to improve in other people! However, while it is right and proper, and indeed expected by the pupil, that the coach should find fault and make suggestions for improvement, do try to sweeten the pill by an equal, or greater, amount of praise. A pupil does not mind continuing criticism, if he gets continuing praise at the same time. A diet of criticism only is indigestible, and equally useless is undeserved praise. So remember to praise, whenever it is possible to do so truthfully, and criticize, when this can be done constructively.

Pupils need to feel confidence in their instructors. It is for this reason that we have set very high standards for our approved coaches; we want them to be authorities on the game, so that people who come to them for instruction can feel confident that their mentors really know what they are talking about. If you are going to teach any subject, you have to know that subject thoroughly, and be able to answer any questions that may be put to you, or at least be able to know where to find out the required information.

Another common mistake made by too many instructors is that they simply issue orders. The orders may very well be correct, and indeed they may seem so obviously right to the teacher issuing them that he does not bother to accompany them with any explanations. He must always bear in mind that his pupils are not as well acquainted with the topic as he is, and something which long usage has made obvious to him, may be far from clear to a beginner. It is always essential to explain why an 'order' to do something is right, and the reasons behind it. Not only will this dispel any suggestion that the coach is a 'dictator', but a pupil who can be made to understand why he should do something is much more likely to do it.

I suppose one of the more common criticisms that can be levelled at schoolmasters is that they tend to over-use their own voices. Perhaps this is simply due to their exuberance at being in just about the one profession where the customer is always wrong! Be that as it may, it is frequently a failing of teachers that they do not answer pupils' questions satisfactorily. They either smother the fact that the pupil is seeking in a mass of words, as they try to explain at far too great length and in far too great detail, so that the pupil cannot detect the wood of the answer for the trees of the explanation, or they assume more knowledge than the pupil actually has at that stage, and instead of a simple answer, confuse him with an over-technical lecture. Another fault is to answer the question that you think the pupil is going to ask rather than the one he has in fact asked. Beginners in a subject can be very easily confused about the most simple things, and one can sometimes be utterly amazed at the apparent stupidity of a question. One must never show this, however, because to the pupil this is a problem, and he has come to you for the answer. Listen to his question carefully, and make sure you answer that particular question directly and simply.

So my basic hints of a general nature can be summed up in the following nine headings:

1. Make your class enjoy their coaching and want to come back for more;
2. Break up the sessions, to prevent boredom, and keep everyone interested;
3. Remember people are visile, aurile or tactile;
4. Encourage at least as much as you criticize;
5. Give the reasons behind your advice, and do not just issue orders;
6. Keep your explanations as short and simple as possible;
7. Answer the exact question you have been asked;
8. Know all the answers and retain the pupils' confidence;
9. Remember you and your class are all individuals; do not become stereotyped.

Now we come to a further nine headings, which apply specifically to Squash instruction. As a coach, one of your main aims must be the safety of the people you are training, and as many of them will have come to Squash from other sports, where the opponent is the other side of a net, or there is no racket to hit someone with, it is absolutely vital at the very earliest stage to stress the importance of avoiding any risk of injury. However a pupil wishes to play his shots, the one thing he must not be allowed to do is swing his racket dangerously, either on the back swing, or far more important, on the follow through. It is also important, as soon as the players begin playing rallies, to explain that there are obstruction rules, and that injuries can occur in bodily collisions, as well as by blows from rackets, and a completely accidental, but clumsy, trip, resulting in the opponent going head first into the wall, can severely damage the wall, and may even do the head very little good! I have found a helpful tip here is to ensure that your players know that they should return to the 'T' from whichever corner of the court they are in by the centre of the court route. That is to say, their first movement after playing a stroke should normally be towards the centre of the court, and then up to or down to the 'T', depending on whether the player is in the front or back of the court. If the first movement is up or down the wall, with the aim of then crossing to the 'T', or even a straight diagonal line to the 'T', a collision is bound to follow very soon after.

In some sports mass coaching is possible, and rewarding. In Squash it cannot be. Well-meaning instructors often try to take on too many pupils, with the result that none gets a reasonable amount of practice or attention, and the lot eventually drift off to the dartboard, pictures or swimming baths. Far better to refuse, reluctantly, to overload yourself, and stick to a number that you can occupy and instruct properly. Obviously the ideal number to instruct is one, but time does not usually allow such an uneconomical use of an instructor's time. However, the maximum any coach can hope to keep gainfully employed is six per court. After the very earliest stages, there should never be more than two players on the court at any one time; but it helps to break up the session if you teach the rules fairly early on, at least far enough to allow the pupils to do a little basic refereeing and marking. One of the best ways of learning the rules is to have to administer them, and this keeps four people out of the six happy at any one time. The other two, knowing they have just had, or are about to have, a go on court or as referee and marker, can be given some Squash magazines, articles or books to read, some task connected with the game to do (practise writing down the score, count up the unforced errors, prepare to advise or criticize the players at the end of the game, etc.), some Squash tests to try and answer, and so on.

The next important point is to make the maximum use of court time. With only two players being able to play at any one moment, and as the whole enthusiasm of your pupils is to play the game, there should be no periods when the courts are not being used. It almost certainly means that the instructor will have to divide his class into two, set one half court tasks such as an American tournament, practice games for particular shots as suggested in Chapter 2, or some other form of exercise, while he talks to the other half. This has the built-in snag that he has to repeat all his lectures, which is annoying from his point of view, but well worth it, if his class are getting the full benefit of time on court. However good an instructor's advice is, what really affects a player's improvement is the number of times he actually hits a ball with a racket in a Squash court, not how many words he has listened to or read.

Another point, often overlooked by inexperienced coaches, is that Squash balls vary a great deal in their performance according to their own speed and the temperature of the court. To give beginners confidence early on and make them feel that they have a future at the game, one clearly wants to make it as easy as possible to hit the ball, and when they begin having games and rallies, they will not, early on, hit the ball as often or as hard as they will when more skilful, and will not warm it up enough to make it bounce satisfactorily, unless the ball itself is a fairly fast one. Although the Yellow dot is used in the major championships, and the White can be used in matches on cold courts quite satisfactorily, it is sensible to start beginners off with the Red dot ball, or even, for youngsters, or ladies with less strong wrists, or under very cold conditions, the Blue dot. In this way, beginners will have a fairly high bouncing ball and will be able to have good and encouraging rallies, which will give them confidence. On the other hand, continually missing a dead lump of cold, heavy rubber is an unrewarding pastime, and very quickly drives the player to some other sport.

It is always a good idea to make practice sessions as competitive as possible. Not only is it human nature to want to do a thing better than someone else can do it, but also it is obviously far more genuine 'match practice' to play competitively. Therefore, when you set your pupils to do any of the practices I have suggested earlier in the book, make sure you suggest ways of scoring that particular exercise. It will be an added incentive to win by doing the practice well, an encouragement for the player who does win, and, one hopes, sufficiently annoying to the loser to make him want to improve. Little competitions add spice to what could otherwise be pretty dull sessions, and are well worth introducing.

Anyone who has heard the average presentation of prizes after a tournament, when the organizers have foolishly elected to have the speeches on court, with the gallery still in their places, will realize that, if one is lucky and the acoustics are good, the audience get at least one word in eight! An inaudible secretary introduces an Illustrious Person, whose name nobody catches, and the latter mouths a few pleasantries, which convulse the secretary, as he is standing alongside the I.P., but do nothing for the paying customers. The lesson I want to draw from this is that it is very unwise for the coach to try to coach from the court to an audience in the gallery. Have them all on court to demonstrate or explain something; be on the gallery yourself, talking either down to the players on court or to the rest of the class with you, but never try to talk from the court. Acoustics in Squash courts

74

are very seldom good enough, and you eventually get a frightful crick in the neck! Of course, it is perfectly all right to be playing one of the pupils, with the rest watching in the gallery, and make brief observations such as 'oaktree', 'blinkers again' or 'too hard', as he does something silly, and you want to emphasize why he lost the rally. I am only condemning actual 'instruction'.

Remember, too, that when your chicks leave your nest, they fly off into the big wide world, which contains a great many different sorts of Squash courts, and an even wider range of playing styles to be dealt with. It is a good idea, once they are able to play a reasonable sort of game, to make sure they get as much variety as you can arrange. Again, the little competitions ensure that they all play each other, and do not just stick with their best pal as their partner all the time. Similarly, if your courts are extremely cold, it is a good idea to take them to a club where the courts are hot, just to see the difference, although it is obviously better if you can arrange a game or two for them under these new conditions as well. It may well be possible for you to create a new team, even if it has to be the club 7th team, or a School Etceteras side, and arrange a few matches against other 7th and Etcetera teams. This not only gives experience of match play, and opportunities to play new opponents on different courts, but just as important, it makes for great keenness amongst your players to be chosen for even such a lowly side as this. The fire of ambition is fanned, and even your biggest rabbit will see his selection as a firm step on the bottom rung of the ladder, which will lead him to the World Championship!

I always feel that it is a coach's job to instil good manners into his pupils. One cannot always succeed, but one can try. I refer to such things as a player remembering to thank the referee and marker after a match for their efforts, regardless of what he thinks of some of their decisions. It is helpful to the officials if a player is prepared to admit when his own shot was down, not up or a double hit, and this sort of attitude usually evokes a similar response from one's opponent,

75

and ensures that the game is played in a pleasant atmosphere. I always dislike seeing players indicating annoyance on court, whether it is with themselves, their opponent, the referee or the Almighty, who tends to get quite a bit of stick from players of all denominations, following an opponent's nick shot! I dislike it for two reasons; one is that it just shows lack of self control, and the other is that it is downright stupid. I am always most encouraged if my opponent starts this sort of thing. If he can be wasting his time selecting the appropriate epithet for me, or wondering if the referee's parents were joined in holy matrimony, he cannot be concentrating on the match in hand, and this will soon go even more disastrously for him as his concentration continues to wander. The opposite attitude has an equally discouraging effect on the opponent. If a player can ride a series of bits of bad luck, poor decisions, broken rackets and so on, with a placid smile, apparently not in the least put out, whatever he is actually thinking, his opponent is likely to feel that such confidence must be well-founded, and that maybe the luck is going to change at just the wrong moment for him. Similarly, it is a wise move to avoid showing any signs of tiredness or distress as long as you possibly can. If it is an even match, both players are probably feeling a bit tired and jaded, and it is most discouraging, when your own legs are on strike and lungs collapsed, to see your opponent prancing about between points, apparently still full of the joys of Spring! Unknown to you, he feels as bad as you do, but is about to win, because you have allowed him to con you into believing you had no chance.

In brief then, as a coach, tell your pupils to try to be poker-faced on court. Tell them to try not to give way to irritation, to try not to indicate tiredness, to make appeals for lets whenever they want to, but always in a courteous way, and not in a manner that suggests that your opponent is a criminal and the referee is his uncle. It is only human nature for the referee to feel better disposed towards a pleasant player than an aggressive one, and this may affect his thinking on any border-line situations that may crop up. And quite right too, though perhaps as a referee, I ought not to say that!

Anyway, it is time now to give you the headings to be borne in mind as a coach for the topics which refer especially to Squash.

1. Stress the safety angle;
2. Never attempt to plan coaching with more than six players per court;
3. Make maximum use of court time;
4. Use a sensible ball for the courts and the standard of your class;
5. Teach the rules and how to referee and mark early, in order to involve more of each group;
6. Make practices competitive, whenever possible;
7. Do not try to instruct from the court up to a group in the gallery;
8. Give pupils as wide a range of courts and opponents as possible;
9. Impress on players the importance of court manners.

I have so far tried to give you some fairly practical ideas about how to set about coaching. There are one or two other more general ideas I would like to put over. I said earlier in this chapter that you have to keep your classes interested and break up your instruction. Obviously the more ways you can think of to introduce variety into your periods with them, the more interested they will be. Sometimes you can give them a talk about the history of the game, or perhaps tell them how it is organized in this country. To do this, you have got to know all about it yourself. It is often useful to invite other coaches or visiting speakers to your club, and ask them to help with your classes. Your pupils may learn something from them, not only because familiarity breeds contempt, and being used to you, they may not really listen as intently to you as to a visitor, even though he is saying the same thing; but also because another person may put a point over in a slightly different way from your own, which makes it clearer to one or two individuals in the class. Furthermore, you may well be able to pick up tips from another person's way of demonstrating or explaining something, which will help you improve your own way of putting across that particular thing in future.

Another valuable aid to coaching is to take your pupils to see a good match or tournament. There is an ever-increasing list of tournaments, and it is possible to see top players in action somewhere every weekend and most weeks. Have a look at the season's programme of events and try to find something to coincide with a course, and get your pupils to see how it should be done. Get them to read some of the books which have been written about the game; once again, in the coaching sections of these, you find another person describing the various points in his own way, and his way may be the magic touch which will open the eyes of someone in your class, and explain away problems that your own instruction has failed to do. Similarly, get them to read any magazine or newspaper articles on the game. This is particularly important if you can find references to either visiting coaches or players they are about to watch on court, as they will be that much more impressed and liable to act on what the famous man says, or imitate what he does. So make sure your secretary or school librarian orders the appropriate books and magazines, and either you or one of your class can collect Squash articles from the papers.

It is also a good idea to show any films of Squash that you can get hold of. These will obviously become more plentiful as time goes on, and as techniques for filming the game improve. Even the early rudimentary attempts are quite useful to a coach, who is prepared to accompany the show with a good commentary. It is also clear that television coverage of the sport will increase considerably in the future, and a coach will, one hopes, be able to draw his group's attention to any programme featuring the game, and, if possible, watch it with them and discuss it. As coaching films become available, coaches must work out their best ways of using these, and decide which will be the most appropriate moment in a player's development to show him that particular reel.

Coaches should remember that they will not always be around to guide a player or class, and should encourage them to join the S.R.A. as members, so that they will always be only a phone call away from a piece of information they need, will get advance notice of tournaments and be able to reserve seats at the major championships before ordinary members of the public, will be eligible to enter all tournaments and competitions, will get a free copy of the Handbook each year, and will be able to vote for representatives on the governing body, and thus have a say in its development and running.

Thus far I have tried to discuss what a coach should do with his pupils and how he should go about his job of improving their play. I just want to add a few thoughts which might be helpful to a coach himself. It is vital to fire your pupils with enthusiasm for, and enjoyment of, the game, and you will not be able to do this unless you genuinely feel those things yourself. It is sometimes difficult to maintain your joy in a sport if you are doing nothing but coaching, so I do advise you to continue playing match, tournament and friendly Squash yourself, and enjoy it, in between periods of coaching. If you achieve any success, it will be noted by your pupils, who listen to you more intently as a result, but that matters less than the fact that you will have 'recharged your batteries' and will come back fresher to your next coaching course.

Take an interest in both local and wider Squash development. You need to know what is happening at the international level, in order to keep your talks on the game up to date; you need to keep abreast of any changes in the rules, because these affect your own refereeing and marking, and your lectures on those topics; but do take an interest in local leagues and tournaments, new courts being built, schools needing advice and so on, and offer any help you can give. For example, with your knowledge of the S.R.A., you could advise any club that is putting up new courts to send the plans for checking to the Technical Adviser before they start building, as we often find it possible to save a club money, or improve their courts at this stage rather than later, after the courts have been built.

It is helpful to get in touch with your club, county or area coaching representative, if you are not so already, and offer to help as far as you can in any courses run by them. It will certainly give you confidence as a coach, if you attend a course, and subsequently pass an exam, and become an Elementary Coach or an Approved Amateur Coach, which is the top award. These certificates are useful, because people can see that you have been trained and are qualified, and because you know for sure that the advice you are giving is sound, and in accordance with what everyone else is teaching! There is also a certificate, following a course, for qualified referees and markers; obviously this gives a coach an extra feeling of ability in this side of the game, and will enable him to be most helpful in all local matches.

So do go on playing and enjoying your Squash, attend courses and pass exams; support the governing body of the game, and things like local tournaments, Squash magazines and new developments and buildings. If you manage to achieve all this, you will be a most valuable member of the Squash community, and your enthusiasm will rub off on those you coach.

5: 'Smith Serving, Jones Receiving . . .'

For the marker and referee

Every competitive Squash match ought to have both a Marker and a Referee, and if this proves impossible, there must be at least one official doing the two jobs. It is unthinkable to have a game of Cricket at any level, without a couple of umpires; it is ridiculous to think of anyone going into a Boxing ring without a referee; I find it hard to imagine any form of racing, be it horse, dog, track or swimming, without a number of officials deciding who won, and who filled the next few places. And yet all too often at Squash, players actually want to play, and are allowed to play, completely on their own, without any supervision at all. There are, I think, basically two reasons for this. Firstly, there is still a feeling left over from the days when Squash was a pleasant and informal affair, that gentlemen ought to be able to sort out any little differences and problems on court in a splendidly British way, and that any talk of needing anyone to arbitrate suggested that the players were unsporting and not to be trusted. Secondly, the jobs of marker and referee are very demanding; not only does the marker's job involve repeated loud calls of scores and other things, but the referee may well have the awkward task of 'penalizing' a player. Once again, in this country, at least, the awarding of a penalty point is only too frequently looked on as an insult to the honour of the unfortunate player, as though he were thereby being branded a cheat, and consequently referees are far too reluctant to award points when they should quite definitely do so.

F

Somehow a few basic truths have got to be brought home to the Squash world, in which even now only the very top competitions provide two officials. One basic fact is simply that now that the game has become so commercial, and the rewards for success so relatively huge, any player's scruples in a vital match are under severe strain, especially if he feels, rightly or wrongly, that his opponent has got away with something earlier in the match. It is vital to have a firm hand controlling such an encounter, in the players' own interests. The trouble is that this extra 'needle' caused by ambition is now spreading a long way down the ladder. With the glittering prizes at the top, each rung on the way up is being contested far more keenly than ever before, and the need to have games marked and refereed well is urgent throughout all levels of the game.

It is easy to see why a neutral referee is essential, even with genuinely sporting and well-intentioned players. There are too many occasions when they simply cannot tell, with the best will in the world, what the correct outcome of a rally should have been. Take, for example, a player who moves up the court to play a ball he can only just reach, and pushes it towards the front corner as a drop shot. He is off balance, and in any case does not know where his opponent is approaching from. As a result, he stays roughly where he is and the opponent runs into him, and of course asks for a let. The striker of the ball has no clue how fast the opponent had been coming, and so probably cannot tell whether he would, or would not, have been able to get it up, or even whether he could have arrived quickly enough to play a winner. Similarly, the oncoming player has probably not seen the ball since it was struck, and has no idea whether it had been a dead nick, and he could not have got it anyway, or whether it had been easily retrievable, or was bouncing about waiting to be hit for a winner. Without an official, all the players can do is agree on a 'let', but if this situation had occurred at a crucial stage in the match, and either 'No Let' or 'Point to the obstructed player' had been the correct outcome, this lack of a referee could alter the entire result of the match. What I mean by 'crucial' above, is 'obviously crucial', such as 9-all in the fifth game; but of course any rally can be the one vital rally on which the result of the whole match will ultimately be seen to have turned. When any game is won or lost 10–9, 10–8 or some other close score, the decisions about 'lets' during the game have clearly affected its outcome, and it is only fair on both players that a neutral observer should have made those decisions. What we need, and need most urgently, is a large number of capable trained officials, willing to take charge of matches in a firm and fair way.

One of the snags in the past has been that, only too often, such markers and referees as we did have, proved, usually through inexperience, inaudible, inconsistent and incompetent, and as a result the players indicated their disapproval and preferred to play without someone messing up their game. The official concerned was discouraged, and did not offer his services again. Result, one less volunteer and two more players suspicious of future markers and referees, and determined not to offer to take the job on themselves!

Because of this suspicion still in the players' minds, the marker and referee must give them confidence in every way they can. This begins by the marker announcing the match in the correct and orthodox way, and throughout the game, making his calls in a loud and confident voice, while the referee is administering fair, and above all, consistent decisions. To do either of these jobs well needs a great deal of experience, concentration and quick thinking. It is absolutely vital to know the rules so thoroughly that not only can the right answer be eventually worked out, but given at once when a particular situation occurs, confidently and in a way that politely but firmly brooks no argument or contradiction.

What I hope to do in this chapter is to talk about the rules, and then discuss the ways in which the two officials should undertake their duties.

Let us start with the more obscure rules, as we have already given the basic ones in the chapter aimed at the beginner. First of all, what happens when a player strikes his opponent with the ball? If this happens as the ball is on its way to the front wall, it is a point to the striker, if the ball would have gone direct as a good return to the front wall; it is a let if it would have been a good return, but going via a side wall. It is a point to the non-striker, if the ball was not going to be a correct return anyway. There are two exceptions to this rule; it is no more than a let when a player is hit with the ball going direct to the front wall, if his opponent has either 'turned' while playing his shot, or it is his second (or subsequent) attempt to return the ball. The reason for the first exception is that whereas it is reasonable, and indeed required by the rules, for a player to give his opponent freedom to hit the ball direct to the front wall normally, the player can hardly be expected to anticipate exceptional actions on his opponent's part. 'Turning' means taking a shot on the forehand in the backhand side of the court and vice versa, having followed the ball round; the direction of the resulting shot is quite impossible to forecast, and it is therefore unfair to add insult to injury by making the player lose the rally after being struck. Similarly, after giving his opponent complete freedom to play a shot at the ball, only to find that he has had a go and missed, a player may find it impossible to avoid being hit by a further attempt. It is hardly his fault that the striker missed it the first time, and therefore a let is the fair solution.

If a player hits his opponent with the ball as it rebounds from the front wall, it is normally his point. The only exceptions here are if it is not entirely the opponent's fault that he has been struck. For example, if he were trying to avoid the ball, but the striker's body was still in the way, and he could not get clear, or if the striker had played at the ball and missed it, or had shaped to play it, and then allowed it to pass through to the back wall, or had leapt out of the way at the last minute. In all such instances a let would be allowed.

We then come to the vexed question of lets and penalty points, and when a let should be granted or refused. What

84

one must remember always in trying to come to the right decision is that the rules exist to produce the fair result to a match, and they can only do this if every rally in that match reaches its fair conclusion. So, basically, one awards a let if the rally comes to an end as a result of some collision or obstruction, when neither player is particularly to blame, and it is fair to both to begin the rally level again. One awards a point (i.e. the rally, not an actual point if the award is to Hand-out), if the opponent is either guilty of deliberate obstruction, or if by accidental obstruction, he has prevented the striker from attempting a likely winner. One refuses an appeal for a let, if the person requesting it would not have got to the ball anyway, despite the collision, or if the collision itself, or his failure to get a view of the ball, was entirely his own fault. This can happen when a player gets himself completely out of position, and rather than run round his opponent to try and retrieve the ball, runs into him, and hopes the referee will give him a let. Or it can happen when a player anticipates his opponent's shot completely wrongly, and claims that he could not see the ball properly, as, for example, if he had assumed the opponent was shaping for a drop, and had moved across to the side wall, only to find that an angle shot had gone across the front wall behind his opponent's body. In order to get a let, therefore, a player must have convinced the referee that he was moving in the direction of the ball at a speed which would have enabled him to reach it in time, and the only situation in which anyone can claim he did not have a 'fair view' is when the opponent has hit it, or more usually mis-hit it, in such a way that it comes back from the front wall and passes so close to his own person, that the fellow asking for the let really did not have time to see it properly and prepare a stroke. The criterion is once again the fair result to the rally; if a player genuinely wrong-foots his opponent, he is entitled to win the point, but if he plays a bad shot, which 'defeats' the opponent simply because the latter was unsighted, he does not deserve the point, and a let is the fair result. Similarly, if a player is

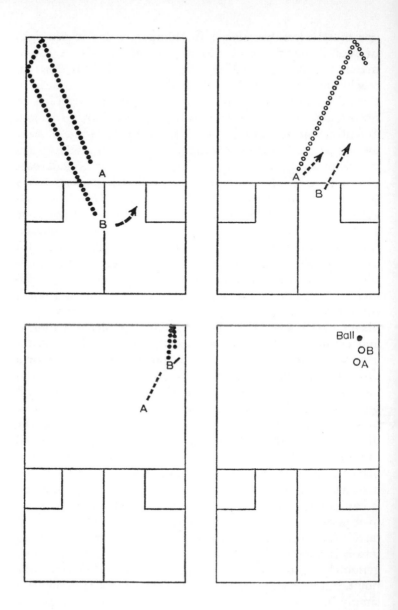

genuinely prevented from getting to the ball by his opponent's accidental obstruction, he is entitled to a let; if he tries to recover from a poor position, caused by his own previous bad stroke, by simply running into his opponent, he deserves to lose the point.

Let us now look at the difficult question of 'penalty points'. To begin with, you must have absolutely no hesitation in awarding these at any stage in the match, any more than you hesitate whether to give a player the point when his opponent hits the ball into the tin. The laws are clear and must be adhered to. Players who take exception to referees giving points against them are either very inexperienced, very conceited or very rude, or some mixture of the three. No one can help obstructing sometimes, usually when he has mishit the ball in some way that leaves him stranded in his opponent's path, and it must be accepted as just one of those things; the normal, pleasant player would not wish to take advantage of a situation of this kind, and the referee must make sure that the ruthless and unpleasant exception to the rule is not allowed to get away with it.

There are two kinds of penalty point; one is for deliberate obstruction, and must be awarded by the referee, whether or not there has been an appeal, at the moment the 'crime' is committed, regardless of whether the other player was in a winning position in the rally or not. The other is when a player has accidentally obstructed his opponent, but, by

---

Figure 5. Accidental obstruction in front of court.

B plays poor shot back to A on 'T', begins to anticipate A's drop.

A plays drop and begins to move in behind B in hope of cutting off his return and covering a counter drop.

B just scrapes ball up, but is carried on by own momentum. A approaching fast.

Point to A. If he could have played the ball, it must have been a winner.

doing so, has prevented the other chap from attempting to exploit a winning situation.

When one refers to 'deliberate' obstruction, the aim is not to make the referee a mind reader and force him to assess the intention behind a player's action, and indeed the rules carefully avoid doing this to the referee in any circumstances. Nor does the rather threatening word 'deliberate' mean that the offending player has to do some dark and dangerous action to be guilty, though of course, any such action would be punishable at least by a 'penalty point', if not disqualification. The meaning is made clear by the words of Rule 17 which states: 'If, in the opinion of the referee, a player has not made every effort to do this, the referee shall stop play and award a stroke to his opponent.' The 'this' referred to is in the previous sentence which says that a player must get out of his opponent's way as much as possible after making a stroke. Notice that the player 'must' get out of the way, and the referee 'shall' award a stroke—not 'must try to' and 'may' —and that the whole thing is left to the opinion of the referee. Thus the rule requires a 'deliberate' effort to get out of the way, and a player not 'deliberately' making that effort is guilty of 'deliberate' obstruction. And do remember that when this happens, the rally is given to the opponent quite regardless of whether he had a winning shot in prospect.

As far as accidental obstruction goes, there are four types of situation, which occur fairly frequently, when one player is prevented from trying to play a likely winner by his opponent's position. The first is in the front of the court, usually when Player A has played a good drop shot or angle near the front wall. Player B has only just managed to scrape the ball up and is at full stretch and off balance. The ball has hit the front wall and come back towards B, who is still trying to recover and get clear. Player A, however, has come up and is trying to get at the ball to play a certain winner to the back of the court, but cannot get his stroke in because B's legs are in the way. A has clearly deserved the rally by his previous good stroke, and it would be unfair on him to start that rally

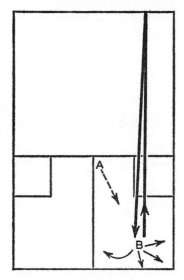 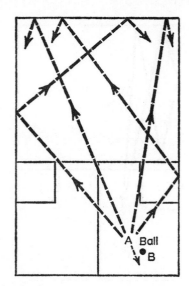

Figure 6. Accidental obstruction in back of court.

B mis-hits a shot back towards himself. A starts moving towards ball. B should move away.

B stands his ground and crowds or obstructs A. Point to A; if B had moved, A could have played drop or angle into the front corner, which would have been likely winners.

again level, so the referee should award it to him. At the same time, it should be noted that B has not done anything unsporting, unfair or deliberately obstructive. He has simply done his best to retrieve a good shot and been unable to do so and prevent himself being in the way; he therefore loses the rally just as definitely as if he had hit the ball into the tin, or failed to get it up before it bounced twice.

The second type of situation is at the back of the court. Player B has hit a ball back towards himself, having aimed to hit it down the wall into the back corner perhaps. He is now required by Rule 17 to give his opponent complete freedom of stroke, so he must not remain where he is, nor may he move towards the centre of the court, if by doing so, he is going to interfere with A's line of approach to the ball. A

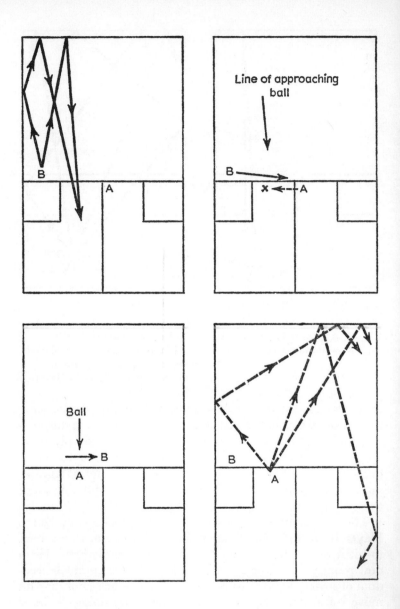

will naturally feel that B should give way towards the back and side walls, and the further he can drive him into the corner, by playing the ball as late as possible, the more likely it is his own shot will be a winner. He is fully entitled to do this, in just the same way that a player must always try to play the ball where his opponent wants it least, and in this circumstance he is only cashing in on the situation set up by B's inaccurate stroke. If, therefore, B does keep out of the way by moving back and to the side, A is most likely to be able to play a drop or angle shot, which will be a winner at the front of the court. Consequently it follows that if B fails to move clear, and crowds A, he must be penalized.

The third, and perhaps most frequent, offence is the jump across the line of the ball. It is also the most difficult to judge. It happens when player B is in the centre of the court, around the service box area or in front of it, aiming to play a shot down the side wall. However, the ball does not go where he intended, and instead of coming back from the front wall between himself and the side wall, it returns along a line between him and the 'T'. His opponent, A, naturally wants to see the ball as it approaches, and equally naturally wants freedom to hit the ball into the open spaces on the other side of the court, and these things he is entitled to under the rules. What he does not want is to find a body leaping across the line of the ball as it approaches, or a body preventing his

---

Figure 7. Accidental obstruction by jumping across line of flight of approaching ball.

B mis-hits attempted shot down the wall so that the ball returns on a line between himself and centre of court.

B moves to 'T' across line of ball, as A moves to position where he intends to take the ball.

Point to A; B is not giving him a fair view of the ball and is probably impeding his stroke as well.

Had B given A freedom to see and play the ball, A could have attempted any one of three likely winners, the angle, cross court drop, or drive into the opposite corner.

taking a normal swing at the shot of his choice, and if B does either, he must be penalized. One of the problems is that B's inaccurate shot may be caused by his leaning away from the ball as he plays it, in an effort to start moving back to the 'T' early, and thus the ball will be chasing him, and as he is already moving, it will be difficult for him to avoid being in the way. However, whether it looks a bit unlucky or not makes no difference. It is not A's fault that B has landed himself in this predicament, and he must not be made the loser out of false sympathy for B. The other main problem is that it depends very much on the speed of the approaching ball, and of B's own movement across the line, whether he commits the offence or not. If his original shot had been intended as a lob, and it is only just hitting the front wall or beginning its slow return flight as he jumps across its line, then he has not impeded A at all, and the referee has to judge the exact moment when a jump across ceases to be legal and becomes an infringement. He will find that this is the situation in which players are least likely to believe they are guilty: I can think of one top player, a noted referee baiter, who is a frequent offender, especially on the backhand, and he always protests most bitterly at any decision to penalize him. However, a referee must realize that if the offending player had remained correctly the wall side of the ball, this would have given his opponent three possible winners, the angle or cross-court drop into the opposite front corner, or the hard cross-court drive into the opposite back corner. He must be given the chance to play these unimpeded.

The final situation is slightly different; so far the rallies have been awarded to a player who, through no fault of his own, has been prevented from attempting a winner. In this case the point is awarded to a player who is refusing to take his winner voluntarily. This is when a player refrains from playing his shot because his opponent is between him and the front wall, and if he did play the ball, it would be likely to hit his opponent. However, this would be his point under the rule we have already discussed about striking with the ball, and the thinking here is that it would be grossly unfair on a pleasant player, who does not want to hit his opponent, merely to give him a let, when the less scrupulous player will have won the rally by going through with the shot, regardless of the risk of injury or the deterioration in the pleasant atmosphere of the match.

So much for 'penalty points'. I would like to deal with one or two other knotty problems, which are hardy annuals in the referee's world. One so often hears inexperienced officials refusing lets because the player played a shot at the ball. Of course a referee must prevent a player from having his cake and eating it too, and basically the idea behind the statement is right, but there are exceptions. Sometimes a player will go up to a ball which is very close to his opponent's body; he can decide to leave it and ask for a let, or try to play a winner, while the opponent is still off balance. If he asks for a let, and the referee considers that the ball was playable, but the opponent close enough to have a putting-off effect, then he will get the let. If he simply goes through with the shot, and hits the ball down, he cannot then claim a let, unless the opponent has done something to worsen the situation he had accepted after he had committed himself to the stroke. I have often seen a player begin his down swing just as the opponent, trying to recover his balance, sticks out a knee, arm or racket, and interferes with the shot, and the referee refuses a let. This is unfair on the player, who is trying to keep the game going, and means that referees have got to be a little careful about administering this particular rule.

Similarly, I have often seen players refused lets because they did not choose to play the ball when they could easily have done so. Again, there is a basic correct idea behind the occasional wrong decision. It is the intention of the rules that the game should be continuous, and certainly that neither player should be permitted to waste time or get illegal rests. It is also the intention of the rules, clearly stated more than once, that each player must have freedom to play the stroke of his choice. Nowhere is he required to play a shot he does

93

not wish to play, because his opponent's position prevents him from playing the one he does. I can give an example from my own experience, when fortunately I had an experienced referee. I was playing a somewhat ruthless 'gamesman' on the fast Bruce Court at the Lansdowne Club. He was a fine striker of the ball, but less strong at the front of the court, and I also felt that I could be fitter, if it came to a long five-game match. Consequently, I wanted to move him up and down the court, and was not too worried about giving him the ball in the front corners. On a fast court it is often easier to make the ball stay near the front by playing angle shots, which slide across the wall than by playing softer drop shots, which hit it direct and rebound a long way from it. He naturally was trying to prevent me from putting my plans into operation, and I found I was getting embroiled in long rallies up and down the backhand wall. I wanted to play the reverse angle across in front of him, to pull him up the court to the front backhand corner, but every time I thought of doing so, I would see that he had moved just far enough back towards the 'T' to avoid losing the point if I hit him with the ball, as he was not quite between me and the front wall, but not far enough to leave me free to play the reverse angle. After I had hit a couple of shots down through changing my mind at the last minute, I began asking for lets. Now, on all these occasions, I could have played the ball back up the wall, whereupon my opponent would have stepped across and volleyed, recreated the position, to my disadvantage, and waited until I took the risk of playing a drop or pulled the ball across court. So it was fortunate that I had a good referee in charge, who realized why I was asking for lets and could see that it was fair to award them.

Perhaps the best advice I can give to any potential referee is to tell him to give decisions which seem fair to him at the time, and worry about which rule he is interpreting afterwards. The rules are there to support the correct and fair result to a rally, and if a referee relies on his own sense of what is justice, he can read the small print later and find out exactly how to justify his decision, certain that the rules will not let him down.

I hope that is enough about the rules, though other details will come out as we discuss the duties of the referee. I want first of all to explain very clearly the difference between the marker and the referee. Briefly, the marker is the man whose voice is heard calling the score and keeping the game flowing, and the referee is the man in complete charge of the match, giving all decisions and adjudicating in any situation where the players disagree with the marker. If he is lucky, the referee may go through an entire match with nothing whatever to do, but this does not mean that he can relax. Any rally may become the problem one, on which the match will turn, and a momentary lack of concentration on his part can be fatal to the hopes of one of the players.

Now, in rather more detail, I want to describe how the officials should carry out their duties. First, the marker. In the minds of all players there is a built-in suspicion of markers and referees; they go on court fearing the worst, and, quite unjustly, they assume that if the marker is not very good, the referee will be equally suspect. There are certain conventional calls, certain accepted ways of announcing things which, if adhered to, give the players confidence, and if not adhered to, upset them and make them querulous. So, although there is no particular merit in the actual words used, there is a great deal of merit in using them in the orthodox way in order that the players may feel that their game is in experienced and competent hands. The marker's first call will be at the end of the knock-up, when the referee, whose job it is to ensure that the five minutes allowed by the rules are not exceeded, will instruct him to call 'Time'. The players know that they have had their permitted time, and must get ready to start the actual match. When they have removed all their coloured tracksuits and sweaters, have spun a racket to decide who will serve and are ready to start, the marker will announce the match. If it is a final, or some other noteworthy event, he will say so, followed by the players' names,

95

identifying them for the spectators by indicating which is Hand-in and which Hand-out, saying what the terms of the match are, and finally the score, which, as it is throughout the game, is the green light for Hand-in to serve. The actual wording of this announcement should always be in the following form: 'Final of the Martian Championship; Smith serving, Jones receiving; Best of five games; Love all.' This, done correctly, shows the players that this is a marker who knows what it's all about, and they assume the referee is equally competent, and get on with the game quite happily. But only too often we have speech making by markers, probably in their desire to be helpful, perhaps in love with the sound of their own voices, and almost certainly influenced by the announcements made from the ring before a championship fight. The players, who want to get on with it, before they get cold, and the spectators, who have come to see them play and not listen to the marker, both want hostilities to commence, and the correct wording of the announcement is the most economical, as well as being the correct, way to do it.

It is equally important for other calls to be made correctly and in the right order. Perhaps it will help potential markers to remember what the order is, if I explain that one starts off with any remarks which affect the call of the score, followed by the score itself, and finally any comments on that score, designed to be helpful to players or spectators. The pre-score remarks may be announcements by the marker that the rally is over because one of the players hit the ball into the tin, in which case the call is 'Down', failed to get it up before it bounced twice, which is 'Not up', or hit it out, which is 'Out of court'. Some markers make the staccato call of 'No' to cover any of these, and this is quite acceptable, and of course, if the end of the rally is obvious to everyone, there is little need to say any of these things, but take them for granted and announce the new score. It is necessary for the marker to repeat all decisions made by the referee; as these clearly affect the score, they precede it. The reason for this is that a referee's decision is either the result of an appeal by one of the players, and the referee's reply, which is a 'private conversation' between them, or it is an award by the referee, because of some infringement, and is again a statement he makes, perhaps with an explanation or warning, to one or both of the players. In neither case will his voice have been audible to the spectators, so the marker will repeat 'Let Ball', 'No let' or 'Point to Smith', plus the score as it is after that decision has been taken into account, in his 'town crier's' voice, so that everyone knows what is going on. As he is required to call the score with the server's points first, he has to change the score round when Hand-in loses a rally; that is to say 2–3 becomes 3–2, and when this happens, he precedes the call of the score by the words 'Hand-out', as this affects his call by switching the actual numbers.

I have deliberately left any comment about the audibility of the marker's voice to this moment, when I want to mention his calls of the actual score, because this is where markers slip up most frequently. You must remember that however well built a Squash court is, it is seldom an acoustic paradise! In addition, the court one is playing on is seldom the only source of noise in the vicinity. Sometimes there are several courts in a row, or back to back, with matches taking place on all of them, and the marker's voice has to be very loud indeed to ensure that at least his players and spectators know what is going on. After all, not only are you battling against poor sound conditions, as well as competing 'noises off', but your audience are behind you, so things are a bit stacked against you! Even at a court like the famous Lansdowne Bruce Court, where so many famous finals have been played, you have to compete with 'tin' noises and doors slamming from the courts above, known unaffectionately in the trade as the 'cookers', and fat businessmen belly flopping into the swimming bath behind the left-hand side wall, and only too frequently does the score echo to row M as 'Splash 3' or '6 slam'. But why I emphasize the importance of audibility while calling the score is because it really is vital to get this over to the players clearly every time. Quite often a player,

G

in the heat of a match, will forget the score, or who was Hand-in and so on, and may play on in an oblivious condition, if he does not hear the score properly. When it does eventually register that his own mental tally and what the marker is shouting are not the same, it is too late to avoid confusion. If he had heard it clearly the first time his own mental tally was wrong, he would probably have realized his own mistake, but later on he cannot recall making one and begins to suspect the marker. The usual reason why the score is called badly is because markers run the words together, and often drop their voices on the second number. One should space the two numbers out, and give each equal volume, which also removes any suggestion of bias towards either player! Thus, call the score 'FIVE—FOUR' and not 'FIVE four'.

Before leaving the calls of the actual score, let us just run over the situation when the score reaches 8-all. At the moment when Hand-in wins the rally, which takes him from 7–8 to 8–8, the marker calls 'Eight all', which tells Hand-out that he must choose 'No Set' or 'Set Two'. When he has indicated his choice, either by word of mouth, or frequently by gestures of varying desirability, the marker will call 'Eight all. No set' or 'Eight all, Set two', and continue to the end of the game in this way. He does not now use the old wording of 'Love all, No set' or 'Love all, Set two'.

Now for the after-score calls, which are the comments on it. Firstly, one calls 'Game Ball' after the score whenever Hand-in needs only to win that rally to win the game. That is to say, whenever Hand-in is serving at '8-something', or at 'Eight all. No set' or 'Nine eight', or 'Nine all, Set two' the marker should add 'Game Ball'.

The marker also calls 'One Fault' after the score on certain occasions. I must explain first that whenever Hand-in serves a single fault, the marker must call 'Footfault' or 'Fault' immediately; the earlier he can call this the better, as it gives Hand-out the greatest possible time to exercise his option of taking the fault or leaving it. If he takes it, he makes it a
98

good service by doing so, and if that rally ends in a let, Hand-in serves again with a clean slate. But if he decides not to take it, before Hand-in serves again, the marker will repeat the call of the score followed by the call of 'One Fault'. It may seem unnecessary at this stage, but in fact if the marker does not do so, Hand-in may not be quite sure why he has been thrown the ball again; he may or may not have heard the original call of 'Fault', and may in any case assume that it was because his opponent was not ready. The call warns him that if he serves another single fault, it is Hand-out. However, the most important use of the call is when the second service has been good, and a rally has developed. This rally may be a very long one, and it may end with a collision, appeals about the legality of a previous shot and so on. Eventually, if a let is given and the dust settles and battle is about to be resumed, Hand-in may well have forgotten that he still has a single fault chalked up against him in this point, that will not be wiped out until the point has been finally settled, however many lets there are before this happens. So the call of 'One Fault' is a very necessary reminder to Hand-in to take care.

Between games there is a permitted interval of one minute, or two between the fourth and fifth games, if the score reaches two games all, and when the referee tells the marker that this interval is over, the marker calls 'Time' to tell the players to get on with the next game. 'Time' is also called during a rally if the marker, or in an emergency the referee, wishes to bring play to a halt. This can be for something trivial, such as the players not hearing a marker's call of 'down', and continuing a rally, which is in fact over. It is more likely to be because a player or spectator has dropped something in the court, which could be a danger, or the door has opened quietly and either of them could run into it. Obviously, if this happens, it is essential to stop play at once, and this is why the referee may well shout 'Time', if he sees the danger before the marker does. The more obvious articles dropping into a court, like glasses of beer, require no call of 'Time'; the players stop at once, but a handkerchief slipping out of a pocket, or a sheet of paper, such as a programme, landing on the floor can be unheard and unseen, but if a player tripped or skidded on either, he could come a very nasty cropper.

That, I think, concludes the marker's duties and calls; they are simple enough to read about, and it sounds easy when you hear an expert doing it well, but are you quite sure that you would come out with 'Let Ball, Nine all, Set two, Game Ball, One Fault', or 'Point to Smith, Hand-out, Eight All, No set, Game Ball' in the correct order, and without holding the game up for ten minutes? Until you can be sure, you are not a proficient marker.

May I ask my readers to study the next few lines in a respectful silence, as I wish to write an obituary following the sad demise of the call of 'Play', sacrificed on the altar of incompetent markers. This, until the meeting of the International Federation in August 1971, was a most helpful call, when made correctly, and I was very sorry to see it go. It used to be made on three basic occasions: first, as soon as the marker could see that the service was likely to be good, provided he and the referee were ready; second, if Hand-out took a single fault; and third, the most useful of all, when the marker either could see that a shot was good, but felt the opposing player might have been in doubt, or when he himself had his view of a dubious shot obstructed, and was virtually saying to the opponent: 'I was unsighted and unable to tell whether that shot was good or not; please play on, and if you win the rally justice has been done, and if you lose it, please appeal, and I will allow a let because of my doubts.'

As far as the first instance was concerned, I always found this helpful. As I said in the instructions to markers, it is the call of the score, which is the green light for Hand-in to serve. Obviously, the marker will not call it, if he and the referee are not ready to adjudicate on the rally, and yet it can easily happen that there is a time lag of some seconds between the marker calling the score, and the actual moment when the ball is struck, especially if one of the players is doing up a shoelace or something like that. It can easily happen that someone, called urgently by the telephone or nature, is pushing in front of the officials along the front row of the gallery, or some organizer has come to ask what the score is, and whether to get the next pair changed, or any other happening, which can prevent the marker and referee from giving the game their full attention. In these instances, the lack of the call of 'Play' indicated to the players that something was wrong, and they should stop play. Now, I presume, they continue to waste their efforts until someone calls 'Time' and stops them. What happens if the service is good and either beats Hand-out, or he hits it into a nick for a winner, before 'Time' is called, I have no idea. Also it is very useful to tell Hand-out as early as possible that a correct service is on the way. Usually he will be ready without the call, but one cannot always see from the gallery, whether Hand-out is wiping his glasses, or the handle of his racket on his shirt, and the call of 'Play' used to give him time to walk away, if he was not ready, and it was then clear that he really was unprepared. Now nothing is said, and the ball suddenly appears near Hand-out, who hastily jabs at it by reflex action, hits it down, and then tries to claim that he was not ready.

The second instance, called after a single fault had been taken, was clearly helpful to Hand-in. I know that players ought to watch the ball all the time, even when it is behind them, and in Utopia no doubt they do. But in real life it does not always happen, and never will. And whether a man ought to watch behind himself or not, he cannot be made to do so, and when you have called 'Fault' early, in order to give Hand-out the maximum amount of time in which to decide to take the ball or not, you should now call 'Play' in fairness to Hand-in, to tell him that despite his fault, the rally is in progress. The call of 'Fault' is still required, but 'Play' is out.

Finally, the call on doubtful occasions during a rally. This was most helpful, and some unfortunate things have occurred since it was stopped. In the less critical case, when a player had in fact got the ball up, but the marker felt his opponent might be in doubt, it made the opponent continue the rally. This could happen on half nicks, and last minute bits of retrieving. It could also help with back wall boasts, when a player perhaps thought he had passed his opponent and had taken his eye off the ball, only to hear the noise of ball on racket and wall. The call of 'Play' alerted him to the fact that the rally was still very much alive. However, the most important case was the one in which the marker had grave doubts about whether a ball had bounced twice or not, or whether it had hit the tin or not, but had been unable to say for certain, as one of the players had obstructed his view. Not having seen for sure that the shot was definitely wrong, he could not call it, and yet the opponent might have been ideally placed to see that the ball was unquestionably down. Human nature being what it is, obviously he would automatically relax, assuming that all he now had to do was to pick up the ball and serve. It is a very rude shock to the system to realize that the marker had not been able to see, and although the referee's doubts allow him to give a let, this is little comfort to the chap who knows he has won the point. However, a sharp call of 'Play' on any doubtful shot, where the marker is unsighted, spurs the player on to renewed action by telling him that the officials were unable to see, and to win the rally outright, he must play on. This does not prevent him from still making his appeal at the end of the rally, if he loses it, but it does give him a chance of actually winning it.

I suppose it is too late now, but I shall always hope that in time the call will be revived, particularly in the latter two cases. I am sure it was a good call, and was only 'sacked' because not enough markers called it early enough, and at the correct times, for its value to be appreciated. With an increasing number of markers, with certificates to give them confidence, maybe it can be reintroduced. I doubt it, but hope so.

Having ground my axe, I will now return to the topic in hand, and discuss the duties of the referee. He is in overall charge of the whole match, and is responsible for its correct conduct and for seeing that it reaches its fair and correct conclusion. He may well have apparently nothing to do at all, but a great many things are his responsibility. His duties begin long before the players go on court. It is up to him to check the little details, which have almost certainly been attended to by the organizers, but which are still his responsibility; I refer to things like ensuring that spaces have been reserved in the centre of the gallery for himself and the marker, that the marker has some spare balls in case of breakages, that the players have been informed which court they are o use, and have been asked to change, and he should know to whom he should give the result, where the first-aid kit is, how long a delay is permissible in the event of injury, whether an alternative court is available, if the match court starts 'sweating' and so on. I am not saying that such things are likely to need checking, but I have known all of them to happen on occasions, and when they do, it is the referee's job to sort things out. It is also the referee's job to disqualify a player who has not arrived within ten minutes of the time the match was due to start. Obviously, if a player has been genuinely and unavoidably detained, one is as tolerant as possible, provided he has telephoned, and the delay is really not his fault, and he is on his way. But when nothing has been heard at all, the referee, after discussion with the match or tournament authorities, should scratch him. Although the referee cannot be expected to be around for an hour before the match, and the organizers should check that players do not break the rule about playing on the match court within an hour of the actual match, apart from the knock-up, it would be up to the referee to discipline a player, who was reported to him as having contravened the rule.

It is also very helpful to the players, if the referee introduces himself to them before the match. Not only can they then look up and make their appeals to the right person, instead of peering vaguely along the whole of the front row of the gallery, but also it is possible for the referee to ask if they wish to discuss the interpretation of any rule; to explain that he hopes they will not hit each other with the ball, as he will award a let or a point, as appropriate, if they refrain from making a shot likely to do so; and in general to get on friendly terms with the two players. This is especially valuable in the case of overseas competitors or players the referee does not know well.

The knock-up has now begun. The referee must time this in order to be able to tell the marker when the allotted five minutes is up, and he must call 'Time' and get them to start play. Normally the players knock up together, but either may wish to do so on his own. He is quite entitled to do this, and the players will then toss for choice of who knocks up first. Clearly it is an advantage to knock up second and be able to get one's eyes used to the lighting in the court, and then start the match, while one's opponent's eyes are still recovering from five minutes elsewhere. If the players do knock up separately, they are each entitled to five minutes, not two and a half minutes each. Normally, when they are knocking up together, the referee will just check that neither appears to be wearing black soled shoes, which are marking the floor, and that one player is not 'hogging' the knock-up by hitting some twenty or thirty shots back to himself before rolling the ball across court, on the floor, to a slightly demoralized opponent. If this is tending to happen, the referee should certainly step in and request a more even sharing of the practice time. He often helps the players by reminding them that time is passing, if they seem to have forgotten to change sides; sometimes, especially under particularly cold conditions, when players have taken quite a while to get the ball anything like warm, they may easily get to four minutes without realizing it, and a reminder is useful. It is also becoming a normal civility to ask the players, as they are changing sides, whether the ball is satisfactory or not. Normally it will be, but if they do want to object, this is the moment to do it, while there is still time to warm up a replacement ball within the knock-up period. At any time, either player may object to a ball on the grounds that it has broken, is not bouncing true or is too fast or slow. Normally, if a ball has been accepted by both players, a referee is not likely to agree to a change being made unless the ball definitely has broken, or is genuinely not bouncing truly. However, if both players request the change, he will do all he can to satisfy them.

The match is now about to start, and the referee must ensure that all coloured clothing has been removed, the door properly closed and that all announcements have been correctly made. From now on, he is in complete control of the match; he must ensure that spectators remain silent during the rallies, that the marker carries out his duties properly, and that he corrects any errors made by the marker, that the players do not leave the court without his permission, do not waste time, do not argue with him over decisions, and that he uses all the wide powers at his disposal to arrive at the correct and fair result to every rally, and therefore to the match. Normally he will have very little to do, and must guard against relaxing his concentration because of this, because at any moment may come the one awkward situation on which the whole match turns. It is a bit like driving a car; very often, if one is groping one's way through a busy town in rush hour traffic, one is forced to concentrate because there are crises every moment, and as a result one has to be particularly alert and consequently avoids any mishaps. On the other hand it is very easy, if one has been driving on nearly empty roads and knows the way well, to let one's mind wander off and to miss the unexpected sudden thing that leads to an accident. Similarly in Squash: if I find myself refereeing a 'difficult' match, I am concentrating so hard that I probably do not make many mistakes, but if a pleasant match is drifting along happily, it is only too easy to switch over to automatic, and fail to see the sudden double hit, or whether an unexpected, and maybe mis-hit, high shot did in fact hit the line or not. Not only may that decision itself prove decisive, but more likely it could, if you get it wrong, have an unfortunate effect on the morale and attitude of the unlucky player, who was concentrating, and knows for a fact that you have done him out of a point. You will quickly discover as a referee that whereas any player must make twenty-seven mistakes at least before he loses, a referee is not allowed even one, because that one opens all the floodgates of wrath, allegations of bias and accusations of myopia, that one can imagine!

The referee is also responsible for the type of match it becomes. A weak referee is entirely to blame if two overkeen competitors turn the game into the sort of thing that normally only happens in Texas bars in films. He has the ultimate power of disqualification, he can stop play and award points and he can, at any time, warn either or both players about their conduct, be it the length of their backswings or follow throughs, their language, their time wasting, their reluctance to accept his decisions, their refusal to get out of the way, or any other action which, in his opinion, is dangerous, illegal or spoiling the game. He is required by the rules to award points in situations I have already described, but he should also make use of his right to warn players; a warning is very often valuable early on in a match to let players know that the referee is aware of certain situations, and will penalize offences as soon as they occur, but there should be no confusion about this. A warning does not take the place of a penalty point, and one does not have to warn a player before penalizing him. It may, for instance, be clear that a player is extremely eager to get after the ball, and is hovering impatiently very close to his opponent, whenever the latter is in front of him. A quick call of 'Time' by the referee, followed by a warning that the player is getting too close and will have to be penalized, if he crowds his opponent, or does not give him full freedom of stroke, may well prevent such an infringement from happening. However, if the player has actually crowded, and not merely threatened to do so, there is no question about whether a point should be awarded or not; it should! And it makes no difference at all whether or not a warning had previously been given. In the event of a penalty point when there had been no opportunity to warn in advance, the referee may well feel that it would be helpful to soften the blow, and maybe prevent a repetition, by explaining to the offender why it had been necessary to penalize him; this is not necessary or required by the rules, but can be one of the ways by which the referee can keep down the temperature of a match that threatens to get heated.

As in coaching, a referee's own personality counts for a great deal. Some, like Chris Campbell, are able to introduce a pleasant note of informality, and can usually chat the players into behaving themselves. I prefer to be rather more formal because so frequently I find I am in charge of a match between players one of whom I know well, and one I hardly know at all. This can lead to the feeling that I must be favouring my acquaintance, if I give the one I do not know the impression that he has wandered into a friendly chat between his opponent and the referee. I also feel that penalty points are more easily accepted, if a player feels they are automatic legal punishments for clearly defined offences, than they are if the referee seems to be giving personal 'this hurts me more than it hurts you' decisions.

To take the extreme step of disqualification, I feel that a referee probably ought to have warned the player previously, except in gross cases of physical violence. I think that a referee should warn a player in the first instance that he will be penalized for such offences as dangerous racket swinging, arguing, barging, time wasting and so on. If the player continues to offend, the referee should give him a second, a very serious, warning, specifically mentioning that any repetition will result in disqualification, and after that, if there is any repetition, disqualification must automatically follow. With the ever-increasing prizes and 'perks' of every sort, players will become more and more liable to the crimes committed through over-keenness, and sooner or later there will have to be a disqualification or two to prevent this sort of thing from happening. There is nothing like disqualifying a player for arriving late for making sure that players arrive on time for the next week or two, and I do feel that it will always be necessary from time to time for referees as a body to indicate that they can bite as well as bark, and I am quite sure the S.R.A. will support any firm action they take. If a match gets out of hand, it is the referee's fault; either he should have been able to curb the unpleasantness, whatever it was, by friendly but firm warnings, and by awarding points, but if normal methods failed, he should simply have disqualified the main offender, or abandoned the match. I recall only too vividly a very unpleasant match in an 'Open' championship some years ago, which was 'refereed', if one could call it that, by a weak referee who allowed a let for everything. In the very first rally, one of the players, well known for standing in the way of his own drop shots, did just that, effectively preventing his opponent from getting to the ball. The opponent, never averse to a good hefty shoulder charge, realized that here was his opportunity and went in as hard as he could, spattering his opponent all over the front wall, and asked for a let. This was allowed, and the game continued with a remarkable mixture of all-in wrestling, advanced second row forward play and occasionally a little scything. The referee ought to have called the players over, awarded a point against the player who had stood over his drop shot for obstruction, and warned the human tank that any further physical assaults would be followed by immediate disqualification.

However, despite all a referee's stern action, forethought, warnings and awards of points, occasionally accidents will happen. Basically, there are three types of accident: there is the one in which a player is entirely responsible for his own injury, the second in which there is one of those collisions for which neither player is particularly responsible, but resulting in one player being injured, and the third, in which one player is to blame for damage to his opponent. In the first instance, the injured player may have tripped over his own feet and gone head first into the wall, and have incurred a gash in his forehead which clearly needs stitching. This is just unfortunate, but unless he can continue play, he must concede the match. This may appear unlucky and harsh, but in fairness to his opponent, who was some yards away when this particular accident happened, it is the only possible decision. Play must be continuous and players are not permitted to have rests to recover their wind or condition, and bad luck or not, this is the only possible answer. In the second case, where the opponent bears some responsibility for the injury, it is a little different. In view of this shared responsibility, the injured player is allowed the maximum possible time to recover, within the circumstances of the particular match or tournament. A player is permitted to leave the club and have any patching up he can get by a doctor or dentist (as in the case of Roshan Khan, hit in the mouth in the Open Championship), and return hours later, or even the next day. If this happens, the game is resumed at the score as it stood when the incident occurred, if play is begun again the same day, but if it resumes the following day, the match is restarted from love all, first game, unless both players agree to continuing from where they left off. In the event of an injury, which the referee felt was the responsibility of the opponent of the victim, he will of course disqualify the opponent, and award the match to the injured player. He need have no mental battles with himself over whether it was accidentally caused or with malice aforethought; it is enough that a wide swing or action has caused serious injury, and this must be punished. Thus, even if the award of the match is made posthumously, it must be made!

I said earlier on that the marker had to repeat all decisions of the referee, and these decisions are frequently the result of appeals from the court. What can a player appeal about? Quite apart from asking for a let—we have already discussed at length how the referee deals with that—a player may appeal against the call of the marker, which alleged that his shot was down, out of court or not up. If the referee was in doubt, or did in fact disagree with the marker, he will award a let and have the point replayed. Indeed, if he was absolutely sure that the ball was good, and would have been an indisputable winner, he can award the rally to the appealing player. Equally, a player can appeal against the legality of his opponent's stroke, which the marker had allowed to pass unquestioned, and which the player thought was wrong. Again if the referee was doubtful, he would award a let, and if he had been one hundred per cent sure that the stroke was down, he would of course award the rally accordingly. If this had happened during a rally, and he had seen for certain that the shot was incorrect, he would have told the marker, who would have called 'Time', announced that the shot was down, and called the score. Remember that the rally is allowed to continue over a doubtful shot, and the referee must remember that the possibly aggrieved opponent may appeal against it at the end of the rally, if he loses it, and if he too was doubtful. A player may also appeal against the side from which his opponent is about to serve, and he may appeal against the call of the score. In both these instances, the referee must decide, and the marker will announce the correct score before play recommences. In other words, all, repeat all, decisions are the responsibility of the referee, and the marker must not interfere. The referee may consult the marker, if he himself had his view obscured, but the decision must always be his.

So much for the normal duties of the two officials. Remember that the referee is responsible for answering any queries about the score or the side from which Hand-in should serve, and naturally one hopes that such queries will be few and far between, because the marker ought to get it right the first time. It is, therefore, absolutely essential that both officials write down the score. No method of holding fingers, crossing and uncrossing legs, or doing anything obscure with toes, can ever be foolproof, and such methods are usually most uncomfortable and unsociable in the narrow confines of a Squash court gallery. Nor can memories, however well trained or used to the job, be relied on. After three consecutive eighty-shot rallies, which have ended in lets, and which have included various appeals about shots of doubtful correctness, and maybe a 'one fault' situation as well, I defy any official to be absolutely certain about the side, let alone the score, unless he has documentary evidence in front of him. It is therefore essential, that the marker writes the score down in order that he can be accurate in his calling, and avoid errors which will cause loss of confidence by the players and confusion on court, and the referee must also write it down, so that he can confidently and correctly answer any queries. It is surprising how a question about the score can immediately make you doubtful, even if, the moment before, you had been quite sure you knew what it was. If it is written down, you need have no fears, provided of course that you have got used to doing this, and it has become automatic and reliable. Do remember always to write down first before calling the score, if you are marking, because otherwise you will have given Hand-in the green light to serve, and he may well do so, while you are looking at your sheet of paper. Also, learn to write the score down in a way which does not require one of those specially printed score sheets, but which will be equally good on any old envelope or diary page that you may happen to have on you, if you are suddenly asked to take over a match. The lighting in the gallery is not always conducive to finding the right little squares to put the numbers in; the particular felt pen you have on you may be too cumbersome for the spaces; you may not always have a card on you; someone has to pay to have the cards printed; a lengthy match may go on over several cards, or a short one may end early and waste half a card. So I am very much against any form of printed card, which I look on as a gimmick, and actually detrimental to one's efficient control of a game. There are a number of ways of writing down the score, which are acceptable, and which give all the information one wants at the time, and from which it is possible to reconstruct the course of the match afterwards. My own method, which many people use and find satisfactory and easy, is as follows. Head two columns with the names of the players, and put ooR under the name of the player who has won the toss and is just about

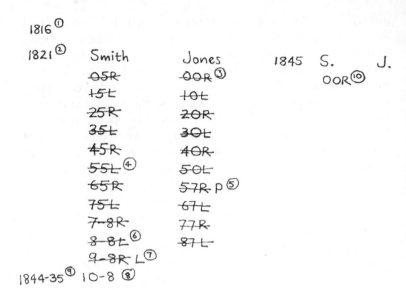

Figure 8. Writing down the score.

1. Note time of start of knock-up.
2. Five minutes later, match starts.
3. Jones has won the toss and is serving from the right. Score always crossed out before new score written in.
4. A single fault, which was not taken. Rally proceeded on second service being good. If that rally had ended in a let, the score would have remained 'five all' and the Marker would have added 'One Fault' to warn the server that another single fault would lose him the service.
5. Rally won by award of a point.
6. Score now 'Eight all' in a No Set or Set Two situation.
7. Rally replayed after award of a let.
8. Final score of game, 10–8.
9. Time at end of game, plus second hand reading for correct judging of interval between games.
10. Initials enough now; Smith continues to serve at Love-all from the right.

to serve from the right. If he wins the rally you cross out ooR and put 10L under it. If he loses that rally, you write 01R under the opponent's name, after crossing out the 10L. It is essential to cross out the previous score each time, so that the one uncrossed-out line is the situation at the start of the particular rally. If a let is awarded, no action is taken, unless you are counting lets for some reason, in which case put a small L alongside the score. If a single fault is served and not taken, make any small mark by the score to remind you to call it, if the rally ends in a let. Similarly, you can put a P for penalty points, and be able to tell avid pressmen afterwards how many you had to award!

I began this chapter by saying that every Squash match ought to have a marker and a referee. I have not changed my mind since, and hope very much that what I have written may inspire some of you to have a go at this very vital side of the game. Certainly it will be of interest to you when perhaps your more active competitive days are over, and do remember one thing in this modern age of ever-increasing crowds, and ever-increasing prices for seats; the marker and referee get seats in the front row of the gallery—free!

6: The Technical Side

'Don't worry old boy; all it means is doing an annual ball test and picking out the one for the Amateur.' Being a trusting soul, I fell for it, and accepted the job of Technical Adviser to the S.R.A. way back in 1957. A few weeks later I found myself discovering what the 'hot seat' really meant, as I was summoned to the great Abbeydale Park Club at Sheffield to take the chair at a somewhat acrimonious meeting involving the club, various architects, builders, plasterers, painters and others, all blaming each other (and the S.R.A. specifications) for an apprently less than perfect new court. Somehow, more by luck than good judgement, I must have given the right answers, but this episode certainly frightened me into learning as much as my strictly non-practical type of brain could absorb about the construction of Squash courts, as well as the problems of balls and rackets. As a result, I have visited courts all over the country since then, trying to advise and suggest, criticize, condemn or repair sick and ailing courts of all shapes and sizes. I have visited the new court built in the grounds of Dunrobin Castle, seat of the Dukes of Sutherland, miles north of Inverness, by the school now resident in the castle; I have examined a court with a 'lino' type floor in a hotel in a popular North Devon resort; I have gone into agricultural buildings, among the mooing and baaing inhabitants, to examine the compressed asbestos sheeting of the walls, to decide if this would be a useful surface for Squash courts. Many is the time I have risked my—to me—extremely valuable neck walking around derelict courts with decaying floorboards and rotting staircase, to see if they could be re-
114

claimed. The R.A.F. seemed to have specialized in building temporary war-time courts, rather less substantial than the ancient mud and wattle huts of our ancestors. One such, in Norfolk, I was highly relieved to get out of, as every piece of wall I prodded, produced a dusty shower of plaster, and a new expanse of chicken wire became visible. As this appeared to be the sole support for the wall plaster, I felt that a sneeze, brought on by the plaster dust, could bring the lot down on top of us. I was once asked to play on a court where the sole source of lighting was a huge searchlight affair at the back of a small gallery. The back of the court was in pitch darkness and the rest of it lit up brilliantly. Apart from a blinding headache and irreparable damage to the eyes, I could see no objection to this, as long as one did not expect to see the ball at any stage.

Recently, of course, glass back walls have required testing. These vary very considerably. At Walton-on-Thames, at the West Surrey club, there are two spectators. galleries at the rear of the court; the lower tier is at ground level, and the upper one in the normal place. This means that the glass wall has a dark area behind it, and becomes a reflecting surface. One cannot leave the light on in the lower gallery, or it would be difficult to see where the wall was, and one would see every movement of the spectators. Initially I found two shots difficult to see; one was an over-hit lob, which hit the back wall on its way down, and it was not easy to judge how far it would rebound, and the other was a shot coming round on to the back wall from the side wall. As the ball came off the back wall, there were two clear images; one was the ball rebounding into the court, and the other was its reflection running along the back wall. The latter had an almost mesmeric effect, and I found myself trying to dig the reflection out of the wall, while the ball was rebounding happily some feet away. I am sure one gets used to this, but of course a glass wall can never be as good a surface against which to sight a Squash ball as can an orthodox wall. However, any minor disadvantages the player may encounter must be nobly and stoically borne in the interests of increasing the game's spectator space, and in particular in the interests of television and filming.

The problems at the Abbeydale Park Club at Sheffield over their free-standing glass wall are a little different. The players do not have the dark mirror effect to contend with, as there is only one gallery, rising steeply from floor level, and therefore a clear and light background to the glass. The main difficulty here concerns the marker and referee. Because there is no upper gallery, they cannot sit in their usual places in the centre of the front row, immediately over the back wall. If they were to sit in the front row at floor level, they would find it surprisingly difficult to see the ball 'through' the players' bodies, and in any case, their voices would have to be 'thrown' upwards and over the wall, and I can imagine even worse problems, when an exhausted player, in the fifth game, was trying to get his point across to a referee with a seven foot high wall in between! The best solution is to have the officials in the centre of row five, 'Wired for sound' if necessary, where they can see more of the ball, and where their voices can carry over the wall. No doubt as the game becomes more sophisticated, and as more money becomes available for experiments, there will be other new developments like these glass walls, which will mean that changes in what is currently considered right and orthodox will have to be expected and accepted. The criterion, as always, must be whether an innovation is for the good of the game or not. Any new idea, which enables more people to enjoy Squash, whether as players or spectators, must be good, and it is up to the technical minds in the S.R.A. to overcome any problems, which it may bring in its wake.

I fear that, over the years, the S.R.A. may have been considered to be somewhat conservative and cautious. I do not accept this criticism; I have, for my own part, always tried to test any new ideas concerned with court construction as early as possible, but sometimes a firm or an individual will have what seems on the surface to be a good scheme for a new type of plaster, floor or whatever. However, one cannot decide whether a chunk of wood a foot square is going to provide the right bounce for a court floor, or a fragment of plaster become a splendid wall surface, without having a test floor and wall built and a proper game played on the court containing them. I always try to get the people wishing to get a new idea of this sort off the ground to put it into a new court at a reduced price, provided I have genuine hopes that it is a sound scheme. This means that the club concerned saves a bit of cash, the firm gets its idea made available for testing, and we may finish up with a good addition to our methods of building courts. Of course, sometimes it takes a long time to marry up an inventor with a suitable client, or the inventor is not prepared to give anyone a cheap sample, and this is where we can be accused of being over-cautious. However, it would be most irresponsible of a governing body to give its approval to every new scheme that came along, without testing it properly. After all, clubs up and down the country are spending large sums on new courts all the time, and it is our job to see, as far as we possibly can, that they do not waste their money. We would be extremely embarrassed, if a club came along and said that they had used a floor or a plaster that we had approved, and it had been a disaster, and we had to admit that we had not even tested it!

On the same topic, it should be clearly understood that there is a world of difference between what we 'approve' and hat we 'recommend'. We must obviously approve anything which makes Squash possible, and which can be helpful to clubs or schools by making courts available, where space or money would otherwise prevent any chance of facilities for the game being provided at all. Thus, whereas, for example, if a school has limited space, a 'foldaway' court in the gym is an excellent idea, and clearly gets our approval, we would not recommend it for a club with aspirations to stage high class tournaments. This consideration applies to most aspects of court building; as with most things, the best tends also to be the most expensive, and if someone comes along with a limited budget, we can tell him how we think he can get a perfectly serviceable Squash court built, and what firms will supply the sort of floor, walls, lights and so on, which he requires and can afford. Obviously, we tend to recommend the firms who seem genuinely interested in Squash court construction, and who have apparently contributed to satisfactory courts in the past, and are prepared to listen to our ideas as to how their products could be even more useful in our particular field.

We have been criticized for having somewhat 'loose' specifications. This is unfortunately unavoidable, because if we made them too precise, we would rule out half the courts in the country. For example, I would love to make a rule that every court should have at least 18′ 6″ clearance beneath all rafters, lights, beams and struts, but I can think of a great many courts which would promptly become illegal. We could solve the condensation problem completely if we could insist on heating for courts being included in the building of them, but this is an expensive item, and would add vastly to the costs of construction, and again, many currently non-heated courts would become illegal.

I have often been asked why a Squash court costs so much, and it is a difficult one to answer. On the surface it would seem that a bare, four-walled room ought not to cost as much as a small house, but there is a good deal more to a Squash court than that. The floor, for instance, has to be sprung satisfactorily, and a correct Canadian Maple floor is a good deal more expensive than most home floors. The plaster, over a very large wall playing area, has got to withstand considerably greater wear and tear than any walls in a domestic, or even factory, situation, and must last for years. The lights, some 18′ or 20′ off the ground, have to be larger and brighter than the one the Joneses have in their dining room, and so on. Add a few bits and pieces like the concave strip marking the out-of-court lines, the flush door-handle fittings, dehumidifiers, the little hatch in the tin for valuables, some mechanism for preventing the door from slamming, a pulley system to lower the lights and save the club Sherpa from having to risk his neck every time a tube or bulb fails, and various ways of making the gallery better for spectators, and you will find that the cost of a court has risen considerably. Some years ago a club in the South London area constructed an extra court at their club, and cut every corner to keep prices down. The end product, at a time when a similar court built elsewhere would have cost the best part of £5,000, was a very good court for only £3,000. However, as any of you who have had to pay for car repairs, television or wireless repairs, watch and clock repairs, will know, it is not merely the expense of the actual materials that puts the price up, it is the ever rocketing cost of labour, and it was this which, by and large, had been eliminated in this case, by using architects, builders, surveyors and so on, who were members of the club and gave their services free, and no doubt supplied what materials they could at cost price.

Many firms and individuals have, over the years, tried major and minor schemes for reducing the cost of building a court, but with little or no success. Indeed, most short cuts prove a false economy in the end, and cost more to put right and maintain than an orthodox court would have taken to build in the first place. No, the encouraging thing about the building of courts is not that they cost less money, but that there is now more money available for them. This is because during the '60s it became obvious that Squash was a game which could be exploited financially, and a club or court complex could be a profitable concern. Not many years ago, a firm in the construction business produced a 'brochure' setting out the cost of building various sizes of clubs, with appropriate club rooms, bathrooms and so on, and giving carefully worked out estimates on how and when investors could get their money back. The final column gave the figures for an eight-court complex; this would cost almost £50,000, which is not a great deal if ten businessmen or firms put in £5,000 each as an investment. The potential membership was worked out in realistic figures per court, and contemporarily fair figures put in for club entry fees, annual subscriptions and court charges. On this basis, it was calculated that the investors would have their money back in seven years, but no allowance had been made for bar profits, fruit machine profits or any takings from meals or any fundraising dances, raffles or anything like that. Bearing these factors in mind, it would be reasonable to suppose that the seven years could be reduced to five or even four with very little effort.

There is also, fortunately, an increasing realization among government and local government officials that Squash is an essential part of every new sports complex, not only because it catches on fast and is easy for beginners to play, but on a more down-to-earth level, it is the only game that consistently brings in a profit and so helps to subsidize the other facilities. So fortunately the desires of the S.R.A. to bring Squash to everyone in the country and the government's desire to bring sport within the reach of everyone are complementary, and courts are being included in all new official sports centres.

It is also encouraging that schools are beginning to make more and more use of existing facilities, whether privately owned or not, and whether the schools are private or state schools. Once again, this means that the courts are being used at times when club members would not be there in large numbers, and so adds to the profitability of the courts, while at the same time giving an introduction to the game to a lot of youngsters, many of whom will want to go on playing when they have left school. This is particularly important where girls are concerned. Up to now, unlike boys, girls have had no chance to play while at school. Only one, or two at the most, private schools had their own courts, unlike the vast numbers of boys' public schools which have them, and the recruiting of girls has been a very slow process. The main way has been via Tennis clubs, which have built courts, or where men players are also keen on Squash and play locally. On days when the weather makes outdoor games impossible, the girls have sometimes been lured on to a Squash court! Apart from that, it would seem that only by having a Squash-playing boyfriend, has a girl been introduced to the game. Now it seems that things are improving gradually.

Before leaving the question of court building, let me say how very important it is for clubs, individuals, commercial concerns or local authorities, who are contemplating building courts, to send their plans to the S.R.A. before they begin to build. This is not to suggest in any way that architects up and down the country are an incompetent lot, but sad experience has shown us that they are not always Squash players! An architect can design a court, within our necessarily fairly wide specifications, which will be an absolute shocker to play in, through no fault of his own. As a non-player, for instance, he will commendably try to save his clients money, perhaps, by building the court with a low ceiling, without realizing how important height is for a good game. We have even had two instances of the floorboards being laid across court instead of parallel with the side walls. In addition, even if an architect does know enough about Squash to interpret the plans and specifications correctly, he may not know all the latest information, which the S.R.A. is likely to have, concerning new paints or plasters, or which firm is now producing the best floors. So we hope that in future we can have the opportunity of vetting any court plans in time to make alterations and suggestions, and save clients' money. It is heartbreaking to be called in to view a finished 'disaster area', which has cost the earth, and which could so easily have been avoided. If the plans are sent back approved, with no suggested amendments, no harm has been done, but if we are not given the chance of helping, it may be that the court will not be quite as good as it would have been. A few days' delay while the plans go to and fro is surely worth it, or alternatively, the architect could meet the S.R.A. Technical Adviser and discuss the plans, or, provided he is paying for the call, of course, discuss them over the phone!

Enough about courts; let me say a few things about the galleries from which misguided individuals actually watch the game. I cannot say very much about the various permutations of spectator seating and standing room made possible by glass panels; this is obviously a matter for each club that is contemplating building a court of this type, bearing in mind the space available behind the panel, how many 'tiers' one is aiming at, and what sort of background the players will have. The orthodox gallery, however, leaves a great deal to be desired, and for a long time yet, the vast majority of courts to be built will be orthodox, and it may be useful to try to make a few suggestions about improving the design of these. Too often a spectator finds himself ten feet or more above the out-of-court line on the back wall, with a solid wall at least up to the height of his waist. This ensures that only the front row of the gallery, standing, can see anything, and anyone behind them can just about see a well-hoisted lob. Ideally, the floor of the front row of the gallery should be sunk below the level of the out-of-court line, the wall should stop at it, and the heads of the seated front row be just over it. This gives maximum vision for them and those behind. It may well mean that players have to crouch as they actually enter or leave the court, but in South Africa, for example, this is by no means uncommon, and is a very minor drawback to set against infinitely better viewing facilities. In my case, it is only a one-way problem; I usually have to crawl out of a court anyway nowadays!

This type of gallery leaves the space above the wall completely clear, but where the floor is more or less level with the top of the rear wall, safety demands bars and railings to prevent people, especially children, from falling into the court. When this is necessary, some thought should be given to the placing of these, and the type of bar used. Obviously safety must be the main consideration, but the thinnest metal bars possible, consistent with security, should be used, and as sparingly as possible. It would also be helpful to see where an average-sized marker and referee would find them least difficult to see round, through or over, and with this in mind, try to leave the centre of the gallery where the officials will sit, free of upright struts. It is also helpful to fix a flat board on the top horizontal bar, somewhere about 5′ long by 1″ wide, in front of the seats for the marker and referee, so that they may write the score down comfortably, and preferably from a sitting position. Not only is this easier for them in a long match, but if they are standing up, they are more likely to be blocking the view of spectators behind them.

It is also, on a cold court, useful to have some sort of heating in the gallery. Watching Squash can be a mighty cold occupation, and there is no reason why it should not be made as comfortable as possible. However, an extractor fan is also useful behind the gallery; this will help to pull the warm and humid air of the bodies in the gallery back over their heads, at the same time, causing a current of air to flow through the court, and these two points will help reduce the risk of condensation on the court walls. Naturally, these considerations only concern courts with outside walls and in cold situations, and do not apply to centrally heated clubs.

The problem of condensation is one which is liable to affect all courts with outside walls, and is one to which the S.R.A. has given a great deal of thought. There are many factors which affect it, and the remedy may vary from court to court. This again is something which clubs ought to take to the S.R.A., where the problem can be discussed and solutions suggested.

Another common complaint is slippery floors. Almost invariably the cause of this is an overdose of 'sealer'. When a new court is finished off, or when a floor is cleaned, a sanding machine is used. This can normally be made to produce three grades of smoothness. The difference between them is only just perceptible to the touch, but can make or mar the final surface. The 'roughest' of the three is the one you want. A very thin coat of sealer is then put on, never more than one gallon per court, and the idea is that the sealer can form its 'skin' below the 'stubble' of the wood, leaving enough wood above the skin to enable shoes to get a grip. If the surface of the wood is completely smooth, or if too much sealer is put on, the surface on which the players are moving, is neat sealer, and although all the firms which make sealers claim that their products are non-slip, they do not say what happens when moisture gets on them. They may quickly turn into skating rinks.

I well remember one occasion when I suffered from this; before the new Edgbaston Priory Club came into being, the old Edgbaston club built a new match court, and the first major event to be played on it was to be the Amateurs v. Pros. match of that year. It had a large gallery, and all the seats had been sold at exorbitant prices, and it happened that Jack Giles and I had to go on first. All went well, though the floor looked aggressively new and shiny, until the third game, when we began slipping on drops of sweat. This got progressively worse until it was downright dangerous, and made our latter games, and the three matches that followed, quite farcical. However, one hilarious moment (from my point of view) happened later in the match, when the floor was at its worst. Jack had played the ball into the front back-hand corner: I had approached it as gingerly as I could, intending to lob it over his head into the back forehand corner, but as I played the shot, my feet went from under me and I fell, fortunately, in a very comfortable position, sitting on the floor, with my back against the side wall, and my racket on the floor a couple of yards away. Somehow I had hit the ball up, but very gently straight towards Jack in the middle of the court. He could have hit it anywhere and won the rally, but as he struck the ball, his feet also shot away and left him sitting in the middle of the court. The ball returned from the front wall and hit him right on the forehead, to my great delight and amusement; sentiments, I may say, which he appeared not to share!

On the subject of rackets in general, it is perhaps interesting to note that Squash rackets are one of the items used by sports manufacturers to work out index sales of sports goods on the home market, and these figures do give a very clear indication of the increased popularity of Squash over the past few years. The figures begin in 1956, when all items, such as Cricket bats, Golf clubs, Hockey sticks, etc., were given the figure of 100, and sales in subsequent years were quoted as up or down from that initial figure, which represented the sales for 1956. At first Squash advanced slowly, but six other items of the eleven quoted also moved over the 100 mark, and it was not until Squash reached 209 in 1965, that it finally moved clear of the field. The advance from then on became so incredibly rapid that in 1971, the last year for which I have figures, Squash rackets stood at the fantastic figure of 919. Of the original eleven items, six had dropped well below the starting figure of 100, and the two next highest to Squash both belong to Golf, with Golf balls at 241 and clubs at 160. I think the figure would be even more staggering, if they had included Squash balls; many beginners borrow or hire rackets, and so the increased number of players is not exactly reflected in the sale of rackets, but every time anyone plays, he has to use a ball, unless he has a colossal imagination!

There are, of course, many and varied types of racket, although the weapons of most sports vary more than those of Squash. The size of the internal stringing area is laid down, and so is that of the framework of the head of the racket, but there are no restrictions on weight, size of the shaft or dimensions of the handle. The handle and shaft may be made of any material, but the head must be of wood. In time it may be that some suitable alloy will be legalized, but for the moment, for reasons of safety, the only acceptable material for the head of the racket is wood. A metal head could be a lethal weapon, if one player were to hit a full-blooded stroke and catch his opponent on the temple, for example. This is a problem that does not arise in the other racket games like Tennis or Badminton, and is a matter over which we can take no risks at all. We have had some peculiar rackets to test over the years; one was alleged to have a soft alloy head, which would not cause any injury. It looked a bit tinny, but I was quite unprepared for what happened, when I idly tapped the wall with it. It promptly went almost square, and every minor bang on the frame was enough to knock it into some new and fantastic shape, ideal for a pop-art exhibition of old bicycle frames, but not the greatest invention for Squash. I am often asked my views on the advantages, or the reverse, of steel-shafted rackets, or in fact rackets with any other type of of shaft than the orthodox wood. Personally, I can see no merit and a good many failings in such rackets. There can be no gain in weight or balance, because a Squash racket is a light article anyway, and even a teenaged beginner can wield it easily, and the point of balance can be adjusted in an orthodox racket to suit the player just as easily as on a racket with a different shaft. However, because a Squash racket is a light article, which can be easily wielded and 'manoeuvred' by the player's wrist, it is, as a result, a less robust thing than a Tennis racket, and in Squash, unlike Tennis, there are walls to hit. This is unavoidable, particularly as one of the main aims of one's opponent is to place the ball as close as possible to the side walls, and to cause it to subside into the back corners of the court. Now, if an orthodox wooden racket, made in one piece, hits the wall, there is the entire length of the racket to take up the shock. It can bend a little, and if it is a well-made racket, is most unlikely to break. If, however, most of the shaft is rigid, the same amount of shock has to be borne by a shorter amount of wood, and must be more likely to break. Even if the shaft is of some less rigid material, such as fibre glass, there are still the danger points, where this is joined to the handle, and the racket head, and it is almost unavoidably at the 'shoulder' of the racket that a break will occur. However well the join is made, it can never be as strong as a solid one-piece affair. My other objection to rackets of this type is that the shaft is a good deal thinner than in the orthodox ones, and when I consider how many winners I have played over the years off the good old reliable wood, I can only pity those who deny themselves this advantage!

The handle is entirely a matter of personal preference, and must depend largely on the size of one's own palm and fingers. I think the widely differing grip sizes of top players is a clear indication of this. My own rackets are of average size, but I do insist on a leather grip. I know many people prefer towelling, and I suppose it does do away with the risk of the racket slipping round in a sweaty hand, but I have found, whenever I have experimented with it, that I could never settle down to the grip as it was always changing. A new piece of towelling would be thicker than when it had worn down a bit, and as it became worn, so did it often become rather 'knotty' and rough, and uncomfortable over a long match. However, this is entirely a personal matter, and obviously towelling will continue to have its adherents; it is just one of those things over which there is no right and wrong, and it boils down to a question of what an individual player prefers, and feels confidence in.

The ball is the final topic in the list of technical items for discussion. It has been the major headache over the years, and if anyone has several months to spare, and is interested, I can give him a blow by blow commentary on all the steps that have been taken over the years to try and produce the ideal ball for Squash. I will spare you even a curtailed version of this, but before you criticize ball manufacture too vehemently, do just consider the problems.

A Squash ball is a very small object, and the slightest variation in the ingredients, or in the way it is 'cooked', is enough to cause it to behave quite differently from its brothers. Rubber is, in itself, an impossible substance to work with; no two batches of rubber are exactly alike in their basic make-up, and as rubber must be, as far as we can judge at the moment, the basis of all Squash balls, we have an unreliable foundation on which to build the absolutely consistent end product that Squash players require. In order to 'debase' the pure rubber, so as to make it bounce rather less, about a third of the total ingredients of the ball may be a solution made of used bicycle inner tubes, or something equally exotic. The more the pure rubber is diluted, the slower the ball will be, but the weaker the fabric of the ball becomes. As the only thing that will hold two rubber type substances together is very strong pure rubber glue, it follows that the slower the ball, the more likely it is to break along the seam. This is because the pure rubber glue is stronger than the fabric of the ball, which tears away from the seam, when the racket hits it at just the wrong angle. This is why, in the days before we switched to the Australian type ball, we were treading a very narrow tight rope between producing a ball which would not break, but which everyone criticized as being too fast, or producing one which people found to be of an acceptable speed, but which was liable to break.

Remember, too, that we are trying to produce balls in four different speeds, which will behave consistently, and satisfy customers who may play on very hot or very cold courts, at sea level or at altitudes of up to 8,000 feet, and who basically play completely different types of game. It is not infrequent to hear the loser of a particular match claim that the ball was too slow or too fast, while of course his opponent thought it was rather a good one!

All I would like to say is that over the years, the S.R.A. and Dunlops have wrestled with this problem, have tried out new types of ball, new ways of making them, plastic balls, different coloured balls and so on. We have visited the factories where they are made, and heard the technical problems of manufacture and testing, and the 'boffins' have come to matches and test sessions on court to watch their products being used. We have never felt we had found the final and ideal answer, and maybe we never will be one hundred per cent sure of every ball, while we are using rubber, but we have certainly done our best, in spite of most players' clearly expressed views to the contrary!

The switch to the Australian ball from the rather spongier

English type has certainly achieved its aim, at least partially. It has speeded the game up, shortened the rallies and encouraged players to attempt more positive strokes. However, with the great spread of the game throughout the world, more new manufacturers are appearing on the scene, and it may well be that in time even better balls, which are unbreakable, cheaper, and suit everyone, will be produced.

7: My Years in Squash

I first went on a Squash court with a ball and a racket at the tender age of twelve. We had courts at Merchant Taylors', but in those far-off days of team game fanaticism, Squash was not really 'respectable', and juniors were generally kept fully occupied building their characters on muddy playing fields. A junior playing Squash was little further up the social acceptability ladder than someone caught smoking, and so I had little opportunity. However, I was lucky to have a keen, and very able, games playing father, and so I owned a racket! It was still in excellent condition, because it had not had much chance to be anything else, when during the war I found myself in the Navy. I did not actually take it with me on the lower deck, for reasons which R.N.V.R. colleagues will appreciate, and others would not wish to, but when I became a midshipman, my racket accompanied me on a most generously planned tour of foreign parts, kindly paid for by their Lordships. By the end of the war, I had played more games of Squash in Colombo, Mombasa and on the old Wanderers Club courts in Johannesburg, which used to be where the railway station now is, than I had in England.

I should perhaps mention at this point that the victory in the Far East was due in no small part to John Horry, who later became Secretary of the S.R.A. He, one gathers, spent a heroic, if harrowing, time in Rangoon, organizing the gin supplies for the wardrooms of the Eastern Fleet. Depending on how you look at it, it was fortunate or unfortunate that, although we were so close for a while at that stage, my meeting with John was a pleasure denied us for some years.

On returning home, it rapidly dawned on me that my naval savings would not enable me to retire, and that an escort vessel's watch-keeping certificate had remarkably little cash value among the employers of Britain, so I joined the academic queue, and went up to Magdalene College, Cambridge. Once again, I was accompanied by my faithful little racket. At last, eleven years after we had first met, we played our first match together! It may well be that a College second team match, in a low division of the league, is not the greatest event, but it was a big day for us! As I fail to recall whether we won or not, I would presume we did not, but gradually we progressed to the College first team, the Ganders side, which was the University second team group, and then the University side and the Cambridgeshire county team. In my final year I played in every University game, except the one against Oxford, for which a somewhat eccentric side was selected and duly lost 1–4, when it was generally thought that there were four other players in Cambridge at the time, from whom a stronger last three strings could have been selected, which would have won 4–1. Two of the overlooked four became English internationals, and the others county players, accepted for the Amateur championship, so maybe we had a point!

However, although I was keen and reasonably fit, I am sure that the thing that gave me my real, lasting, interest in the game was the influence of John Readwin in the Cambridgeshire side. He was one of the most complete games players there can ever have been, he played for various counties at Cricket, Tennis and Squash; he was an excellent golfer, a superb rifle shot, and it was a brave man who risked a beer on a darts match with him. The great thing about him was that one simply could not conceive of John playing any stroke at any game ungracefully. At Squash he had a wonderful range of shots, and was virtually unbeatable on the very cold courts in Cambridge. Certainly, ever since those days, I have tried to play a variety of shots (though never achieving the Readwin gracefulness, I admit) and have preferred that style of play to the ultra-defensive game, based on fitness and retrieving, in which the player takes no risks himself, and simply hopes his opponent will do all the attacking, and run out of ideas, luck and breath.

It occurs to me that I have been extremely lucky in all the teams I have played for, whether it was Cambridgeshire in the early 1950s, or Middlesex after that, the M.C.C. in the Bath Cup, the former Hampstead Squash and Rugby Fives Club in the Cumberland Cup, the Old Merchant Taylors' in the Londonderry Cup, not forgetting the touring sides I have been overseas with. Of course, with so many people playing Squash, and with the physical contact side of things encouraging the unscrupulous player to indulge in a bit of unpleasantness, there are bound to be some who do not endear themselves to their fellows as much as others. But this applies in all games, and I think Squash players are a remarkably pleasant bunch of people. This becomes even more apparent when one goes to a course at one of the big sports centres, and sees what other sports have to put up with! Certainly I have had some terrific team mates and friends in Squash, and in recent years have found new but equally valued friends among people I have met in my various wanderings around the county as Technical Adviser of the S.R.A. or Director of Coaching.

These two jobs were another example of my good luck in the game. I was a very junior committee member in 1957 when the technical job became vacant, and it was by pure chance, or some act of God or Horry, that I was asked to do it. As far as the coaching job went, this was offered around to several people, before I was asked to have a go, so it was my good fortune that the others did not have time to undertake it.

On the technical side, I have had great help and sound advice from Desmond Morris, who always answers any queries on the architectural side of things. I remember the Engineer Officer on the *Vanguard* used to have four trays on his desk, instead of the usual three. These were marked 'In', 'Out', 'Pending' and 'Too Bloody Difficult'. Mr Morris has always kept my 'trays' down to three; anything that would have been put in the fourth has gone straight to him. In more recent years, I have also had a great deal of help from Arthur Boyse, the Squash dynamo of the Midlands. It is always pleasant when one actually likes the people one has to deal with, and I have always very much enjoyed the company of Messrs. Morris and Boyse.

It has been the same, I am glad to say, on the coaching side of things. In the first instance, the job of Director of Coaching was created in order to try to solve the problems of the lack of coaches in the country. Clearly, there was, at that time, no prospect of sufficient money being forthcoming to induce vast numbers of potentially good coaches to turn professional, so one had to think in terms of amateur coaches. Equally, we wanted these amateurs to give much of their time to this task, and we realized that many might well be people who needed to earn a little extra cash over and above their normal salaries, and if they devoted much of their spare time to coaching, they would not be able to do this. But we needed them, and the knowledge they had, or were prepared to acquire, and so we had to accept the revolutionary fact that we had to create a new animal, the Approved Amateur Coach, who would actually receive money for coaching! On the face of it, such a proposition could obviously expect hostility from the existing Professionals, although we felt, rightly as it turned out, that anything done to spread the game, popularize it, attract people to it and satisfy the demand that the Professionals simply could not begin to cope with, would, in the long run, benefit them, as much as anyone else. Initially, however, it took a man of considerable perception and generosity to persuade his fellow Professionals that this was so, and indeed to take the major part in all subsequent courses instructing these would-be Amateur coaches, and in their examination. I refer, of course, to Jack Giles.

In these past ten years I had had a great deal to do with Jack; we planned the initial courses and exams together, and we have been together on all but one or two, discussing how the courses could be improved, or whether we ought to pass or fail some borderline examinee. I am glad to say I have seldom met a character with a bigger fund of unrepeatable stories, a nastier habit of telling his shady R.A.F. reminiscences of the war as you are flying on an uneasy stomach over the North Sea, or an equal knack of producing, out of a completely dead-pan face, some quiet, hysteria-inducing crack, at a moment when a straight face is essential. He is, without any doubt, the finest Professional this country has ever produced; he might or might not have beaten Barrington had they been contemporaries, but in his contribution to Squash he is certainly tops in my book! My own generosity shines through these remarks, as you will realize when I tell you that when we were in Stockholm, lecturing and examining the Swedes (male, dammit!), it was suggested that we should try the English pub there. Jack manoeuvred it that I got to the bar first, as usual, but when a round of a half of Guinness and a pint of bitter came to over thirty bob, it was made very clear that his round would follow at a rather later date!

Amongst our Amateur coaches, we have certainly produced a number of men who have done a tremendous amount of work, and whose influence has produced great results in their own areas. It is invidious to select people for special mention, but my Honours List would certainly include John Pugh, Howard Kirby, David Richardson, Geoff Pike, Norman Rosser and Brook Oldman. It is no coincidence that Squash, and in particular Squash coaching, is flourishing in their areas.

I have found, since I became involved in coaching, that there are considerable differences of opinion on the best ways and means to put various things across, whether it is the perfection of a stroke, tactical thinking, refereeing and marking or any other aspect of the game. I know that I am learning all the time, and have frequently found most ingenious and helpful ideas from people attending coaching courses and exams—either from their answers to our written papers or in general conversation. In the written papers, I find an enormous range of answers. Once, I remember, I asked what a coach should do if he found that a beginner was having great difficulty in hitting the ball at all, whether it was dropped for him, hit gently towards him or anything else. One gentleman, who had clearly encountered the problem, suggested that the pupil should be encouraged to transfer his attentions to some other sport, and specified darts, which I felt could be dangerous! Another, perhaps judging others by himself, said he would wait until the chap sobered up. A Naval officer said he would send him to the oculist, and there were all the usual theories, and all different, about grip, foot position, which muscles should be tensed and which tendons relaxed. The answer (to avoid a flood of mail from eager questioners who may encounter the same problem—as coaches, not players, of course!) is to get the rabbit to hold his racket out, and as he is finding it difficult to make contact with the ball, do it for him by placing the ball on his racket, and telling him to balance it there. As he does this, his eyes will get used to focusing the ball on the racket, which will help them direct the racket head at the ball when next it aims at it, and his arm and hand will get the 'feel' of the racket actually succeeding in doing what it intends to do. When the player has kept the ball on the racket for a few minutes, and been duly congratulated and encouraged on this feat, make him bounce it up and down very gently, still making sure it does not fall. Gradually increase the height of the bounce until the player can do this competently, and then take him to a wall, while he is still bouncing the ball on his racket, and from quite close to the wall, get him to begin tapping the ball on to the wall, and you have won! If he still cannot do it, then is the time to suggest darts, fruit salts or the oculist!

To return to my own playing days, after I left Cambridge I went back to Merchant Taylors' as a master. Squash was still an 'unofficial' sport, with no matches, and the O.M.T.s did not even enter for the Londonderry Cup, and had no coach at that time. Luckily, my first school captain was Colin Burrell, whose father, also an O.M.T., was a keen Squash player at the Henley club, and we arranged a few 'unofficial' fixtures. Gradually things developed along the right lines, and I had some useful players like Robert Montgomerie and Chris Harding, both subsequently Oxford 'Blues', to help build up the school's reputation. I had begun playing for the Hampstead S. & R.F.C. in the Cumberland Cup, and was tearing all over London in the evenings and weekends playing in every tournament I could get to. Eventually, in 1953, at the somewhat ripe age of thirty, I played for England. This was a great thrill, of course, but my excitement turned to mirth when my Scottish opponent, who had never played on anything warmer than the Edinburgh courts, came up to me at the end of the knock-up on the R.A.C. No. 2 court, and remarked, with a dazed expression on his face, that I could have him with chips in about eight minutes!

In 1955 the first British side to tour abroad since the trips to North America in the 1920s was invited to go to South Africa. At this time, selection of the England side left much to be desired; many of us in or near the team had resented for years the way in which certain veterans seemed to be automatic selections for the internationals, without being required to prove their current form against the young contenders. In those days, there was no recording of all results, and no reporting back to an overall committee of the deliberations of the selectors. How the selectors themselves were chosen was a deep mystery, and there were frequent instances like the occasion when a selector appeared at the Amateur, and asked a friend of mine the name of a certain player on court. The player happened to be one of the current England side!

Following my long stays in South Africa during the war, I was naturally very keen to go on this tour, and had a pretty good season. In league and championship Squash throughout the season I had lost only to Alan Fairbairn and Roy Wilson, though I had not played Alan Seymour-Haydon, and would not have reckoned to beat him. Before the team was selected, it was announced that neither Fairbairn nor Wilson was available. Seymour-Haydon was among the five men selected, but it was not only disappointment that led me to do the 'unspeakable' and query the selection of the rest of the team. Initially I was told quietly that one cannot do that sort of thing. Off the record, I was told that the selectors felt we did not need our strongest side to beat the South Africans, as their champion, David Hodgson, was in England and they considered that this side would be good enough. What they had not bothered to find out was that when Hodgson had won the South African championship it was held in Rhodesia, and none of the current Transvaal side had been able to play. The South African team, with the two Callaghan brothers, Brian and Denis, Cecil Kaplan, Roger Jarvis and Tony Barnes, were a combination we possibly could not have beaten anyway without Fairbairn and Wilson, but as it was, we virtually gave them the series.

Anyway, unknown to me, apparently a good deal of feeling had been aroused, and an anonymous, very generous minded man organized a fund to send a sixth player on the tour, so I was fortunate enough to go after all. I think my point was made when the South Africans came back to England a year and a half later, and with Great Britain at full strength, I was selected as one of the three home players, and we got our revenge for the defeats on the tour. There will always be dissension over selections in Squash, because clashes of style mean that results are in themselves inconclusive, and obviously when selectors have to pick one player from two or three equally well qualified candidates, the unlucky ones often see this as an injustice. Nowadays, however, the system is as fair as it can ever be. The selectors include men from areas outside London, or men detailed to study results from certain parts of the country, and a chart of all available results between the top twenty or thirty players is kept in the

S.R.A. office. Any apparently blatant unfairness would cause a storm of protest in a Squash publication, and all in all, everything is now done much more 'professionally', if one dare use the word!

In 1960, I skippered the first ever club Cricket side to tour South Africa, and during this Romany tour, I met Kendal Jarvis, the younger brother of my old friend and foe from the two Squash series, Roger Jarvis. He told me he was considering starting a club to benefit up-and-coming, promising young players, and felt it would be greatly to their advantage if they could do a tour of the U.K. He asked me if I would undertake the arrangements for matches, accommodation and travel at the British end, and naturally I agreed. The first team arrived twelve months later, at the end of November 1961, and the tours have continued every two years since then. It is evident that the aim of the Knights club has been fulfilled, as all South African international teams contain a high percentage of players who have been on these tours, and in fact, of the twenty players appearing in the unofficial ranking list in the South African Tennis and Squash magazine, usually as many as seventeen are Knights. They have always proved very welcome and pleasant visitors, and their tours have been as successful off the court as on it, which is saying something! The Knights also invite back to South Africa a British side, which I select from among the more promising young players in the U.K. We do not tour as often as the Knights, because our young players do get a wide range of tournament play and practise at home, and finance is usually a greater problem, but when circumstances are right, and there are some suitable candidates, another Swallows team flies South. When asked, on our first tour, why we chose the name 'Swallows', we explained that they were English birds that flew South; the word also indicated what we intended to do to South African beer and that we were interested in other 'birds', not to mention what we aimed to do to our South African opponents as we flew over them!

Some years ago I was also asked by the coach of the University of Pennsylvania, Al Molloy Jnr., to arrange a tour for his Squash players. This was a tremendous success. Not only was their standard of play very much higher than we had expected, but they were a very good crowd, and obviously went back home devoted fans of the British game. A second tour three years later was equally successful, and these young Americans could well be the foundation on which future G.B./U.S. relations are based. They have proved that Americans can enjoy our game, and that it not only does no harm to their play at their own game, it is of positive benefit. The first touring side returned home to an all-conquering season. This bears out what I have always felt; the games are too different to try to amalgamate them, but sufficiently alike to be mutually helpful, existing side by side, just as Squash and Rackets pursue their parallel paths in this country. Certainly, I am very much against messing around with the rules, court dimensions, methods of scoring or the respective balls of the two games. All that one would do, if this were pursued, would be to produce a third game, inferior to either of the originals.

The 1960s saw great changes in the administration of the game. First of all, the S.R.A. put its own house in order. I had a certain amount to do with this, as I wrote a 'thesis' on the inefficiency of the set-up, copies to all and sundry, with suggestions as to how things could be improved and streamlined. These suggestions were adopted, pretty much as I had proposed, and the organization I described earlier in the book came into being. The main reason a change was needed was the enormous growth of the game overseas, and the vastly increasing number of tours abroad, visiting teams and players coming to this country, and general exchanges of views about the rules and equipment. Prior to this reorganization, the game had been run in this country largely by the Finance and General Purposes Sub-Committee. On the whole, this worked well enough, but it was not a senior enough body, or sufficiently 'high powered' and experienced, to take really important decisions on its own, and it had to refer back to the large Executive Committee, which met very infrequently. It was becoming clear that a small 'action' committee was needed, fully empowered to take decisions, and engage in the necessary quick-fire dialogue with other governing bodies, and so the Management Committee was created, responsible to the Council and elected annually.

My efforts to get this more modern organization introduced were not meant to be critical of the F. & G.P. Sub-Committee, which had done a good job. It was simply one of the earlier steps necessary to make the S.R.A. a more efficient body, capable of dealing with a rapidly developing world sport. While it is certainly true that in my earlier years in Squash there was a certain amount of 'dead wood' at the top of the organizing tree, very happy to see the game trundle along as it always had, as the sport for Public Schools and Universities, there were also many far-sighted committee members, who saw how things were developing, and who were prepared to devote a lot of time and energy to helping things go along the right way.

It is always very easy to criticize the establishment, and assume that anyone over sixty is senile and useless, but if and when some of the critics are prepared to come and serve on sub-committees, they may be very grateful for some of the experience and goodwill available from the despised elder statesmen! For instance, over the years as Technical Adviser, I have had situations where I have needed help, advice or support, and always found the then President of the S.R.A., Colonel Philip Le Gros, a remarkable ally. He never forced his advice on anyone, but if asked, gave very sound counsel indeed, and was prepared to go to considerable trouble himself to support one of his junior colleagues.

Of course, it just is not possible to talk about the development of Squash without mentioning John Horry. He was made Secretary just when the first overseas tour to South Africa had taken place, in 1955, and remained in office until 1972. It was incredibly fortunate for Squash that someone of

140

his tremendous energy and enthusiasm should have been available during these all-important years. At times the avalanche of work resulting from the 'boom' in the game all but overwhelmed the little amateur organization that the S.R.A. had always been, and many of us, who had had small committee tasks before all this began, found we were virtually doing a second full-time job, but in the centre of everything there was always John. He and I have had many disagreements, but no two people determined to get things done will always see eye to eye on the best ways to do them, and we have certainly never had a real quarrel. I have been, and am, most grateful for all the help and advice he has given me over the years, and for the kindness and generosity which so many of us have enjoyed.

After dropping out of the England side at the ripe young age of thirty-seven, I continued to play for Middlesex in the inter-county championship until I was forty-six, and even longer in the Bath Cup for M.C.C., but at forty-five I swallowed my pride and entered for the Veterans Championship, and managed to win it, and continued to do so for a few years, although it becomes more and more difficult each year to withstand the challenge of the young striplings of forty-five who come fresh, slim and virile to attack their elders. It always seems that more people watch the older veterans' matches, and I liked to think this was because our splendid stroke play was pulling them in, but I have begun to get a nasty feeling that the extra spectators are doctors, undertakers and matrons of geriatric nursing homes, waiting, and indeed vying, for our custom if the worst should befall us on court!

It would be only too easy to go on reminiscing, but the game of Squash is looking ahead, not backwards, which is only right. The boom is by no means finished yet, nor will it be until there are sufficient courts in every town and village in Britain to enable everyone who wants to play to do so. And even then, the development must continue abroad; a game which can flourish in England, Sweden, India, South

Africa, Australia, New Zealand and Japan can clearly flourish everywhere, and it is up to us, and the International Federation, to give all the help, encouragement and advice that we can to countries who are beginning to play.

I hope films and television programmes about Squash become commonplace, instead of none-too-satisfactory rarities. Clearly, we have much to learn about this, and we have to work in very close harmony with film experts to make Squash worthwhile on a screen. Not only have the pictures themselves got to be clearer, but commentaries, descriptions and explanations must improve.

I would like to thing that the next few years will see a flood of superb markers and referees leaping forth to handle the most awkward games with firmness, tact, consistency and charm, but I know this will be an uphill struggle for a long while yet.

Finally, I hope that however competitive the game becomes—and it will get more and more cut-throat as prizes increase and the rewards for winning become more attractive —the leading players will remain aware of the responsibility they have to set a good example. It can only do the game harm if a well-known player behaves like a spoilt child when some decision goes against him, showing annoyance with himself, the referee or his opponent. Equally, any forms of sharp practice or gamesmanship are very quickly imitated by inexperienced players, who assume, not unreasonably, that if A can get away with it, they can. If the leading players behaved correctly, courteously and fairly, this would do a great deal of good for the game. No player is bigger than the sport, however inflated his ego may have become after a run of success, and it is surely better to achieve something for the game, as well as at it.

Certainly, I envy the young men of today; my generation had a good run for its money, but the opportunities are so much wider now, and the future so exciting and promising, that I would certainly like to be an 'up and coming' player at the moment. I hope the game will continue to develop and give pleasure to thousands, even millions, of future Squash addicts, and I hope I shall be around for a while yet, playing in the old men's events, and helping the S.R.A. to tick over!